King David Speaks from Heaven

A Divine Revelation

Matthew Robert Payne

This book is copyrighted by Matthew Robert Payne. Copyright © 2018. All rights reserved.

Any part of this book can be photocopied, stored, or shared with anyone for the purposes of encouraging people. You are free to quote this book, use whole chapters of this book on blog posts, or use this book for any reason to spread the message of Jesus to this world. No consent from the author is required.

Please visit http://personal-prophecy-today.com to sow into Matthew's writing ministry, to request a personal prophecy or life coaching, or to contact him.

Cover designed by akira007 at fiverr.com

Edited by Lisa Thompson at www.writebylisa.com You can email Lisa at writebylisa@gmail.com for your editing needs.

All scripture is taken from the New King James Version unless otherwise indicated. Copyright © 1982 by Thomas Nelson, Inc. Used by permission. All rights reserved.

The opinions expressed by the author are not necessarily those of Christian Book Publishing USA,

Published by Christian Book Publishing USA,

Christian Book Publishing USA is committed to excellence in the publishing industry. Book design Copyright © 2018 by Christian Book Publishing USA. All rights reserved.

Paperback: 978-1-68411-541-9

Hardcover: 978-1-387-70703-4

Dedication

This book is dedicated to three women who I love and admire: Rebecca, Mary, and Nicola.

Rebecca:

I am so pleased that I have met you. You have been a good friend to me, and I look forward to getting to know you better.

Mary:

You are a joy to me. You have provided me with many hours of great conversation, and you have spent many hours reading my books. You are proof that a reader can become very close friends with an author.

Nicola:

You are my beloved friend. We used to talk once a week, and now we talk more often. Your prayers bring breakthrough in my life. You mean a lot to me.

I want to thank you all for providing me with the questions to ask David. I hope that you enjoy his answers to your questions and that you enjoy the whole book. All of you were once only readers of my books, and now you are very close to me.

Acknowledgments

I want to thank Jesus for the relationship I have with him. You have faithfully been with me through all of my life. Son of David, you must be happy about seeing this book produced. I honor you and will always do what I feel you call me to do.

I want to thank God for loving me and for giving me his Son to be my best friend. Through the years, I have become closer to you. In the *Conversations with God* series, I have been able to record some of our two-way conversations. Thank you for my life.

I want to thank the Holy Spirit for guiding me and keeping me on the right track. Thank you for helping me to write my books.

I want to thank Bethany, my scribe angel. You do a wonderful job in my life. I cannot wait till I can see you more clearly, and I am able to give you a big hug. I love the work that you are doing with me.

I want to thank King David for coming down and being so open and honest with this interview. I have learned a lot about you through this book. It's awesome to live a life of no regrets.

I want to thank Lisa Thompson, my copy editor. You can contact her at writebylisa@gmail.com I want to thank Nicola for proofreading my books and for catching the tiny details to make them a true work of excellence.

I want to thank Mary, Nicola, and Rebecca for giving me questions to ask David.

Special love goes out to my parents, Bob and June Payne, who love me with a remarkable love.

Thanks to Bill Vincent of Revival Waves of Glory Books and Publishing, who helps me publish my books.

I want to thank my readers. You give me something to do and also give me great feedback.

I want to thank all my ministry supporters who have sowed into my ministry, including the anonymous supporter of this book. Without you, I could not produce so many books. You know who you are!

I want to also thank my friends, David Joseph and Michael Van Vlymen, who have shown me what excellence in writing looks like.

Introduction

How does one sit down and interview one of the greatest saints in the Bible? How does one get that opportunity? I think Jesus was simply looking for a person who would dare to do so.

You will read some things in this book that might shock you. I know that I was shocked. That is natural for us as we are carnal. David is speaking from a place of love and security in Jesus Christ.

I originally asked six people for the questions for this book, and yet after the three women replied to me, I knew that twenty-eight questions from them were more than enough. David's life is such a big subject that I am sure we could have had a hundred questions and not have exhausted his life.

It is my prayer that you enjoy this book.

Table of Contents

Dedication 3

Acknowledgments 4

Introduction 6

Matthew's Question 11

Question 1: How do you feel about being here today, David? 11

Nicola's Questions 14

Question 2: What were your thoughts when you were dancing before the Ark of the Lord? How did it affect you when Michal despised your dancing? 14

Question 3: How did you feel about the trouble with your sons, especially Absalom and Amnon? What would you have done differently in how you handled them? 16

Question 4: After you succeeded in life and had so much victory in battles, what was it like to deal with Saul's jealousy of you? 19

Question 5: Why did you have so much love for those who did you wrong, including Saul and others, despite how they treated you? 21

Question 6: Ziklag was destroyed by fire, and your men's wives and children were stolen. When you and your men came to Ziklag, the men were talking of stoning you. The Bible says that you "found strength in the Lord" (1 Samuel 30:6). What did God say to you at that time, and how did you encourage yourself? 23

Question 7: You are the famous writer of the Psalms, which are still being put to music today. What would you say to Christian songwriters of our day?... 26

Question 8: What do you have to say about your friendship and love for Jonathan and his crippled son, Mephibosheth? 28

Mary's Questions... 32

Question 9: Can you describe what it felt like to be called a man after God's own heart? 32

Question 10: What advice would you give to someone who has committed adultery or who is thinking about committing adultery? Or someone who's currently committing adultery? 34

Question 11: What chapter in the book of Psalms encouraged you the most? 36

Question 12: When you realized God was not going to allow you to build the temple but that it would be built by your son Solomon, how did you feel about that? 38

Question 13: Can you describe the happiest moment of your life? 41

Question 14: What advice do you have for Christians in 2018 who are trying to live for the Lord but who are being attacked by the enemy? . 43

Question 15: Can you describe the pride you feel in knowing that Jesus referred to you as the son of David in the Bible?................................... 45

Question 16: What is your favorite thing about heaven, and what are your favorite things to do there? 47

Question 17: Can you describe how you felt when you were anointed king of Israel at such a young age?... 50

Question 18: Why do you think King Saul eventually agreed to let you fight Goliath? 52

Question 19: Can you describe your greatest accomplishment as the king of Israel? 54

Question 20: Can you describe the darkest hour of your life? What advice can you give people today on how to overcome heartaches, trials, and attacks from our enemies? What advice do you have for someone who suffers from depression? 56

Question 21: If you could live your life over again, what would you change and do differently? 59

Question 22: What was the biggest impact playing music and singing had in your life? 61

Question 23: What advice can you give Christians who are trying to live a holy life for God today? 63

Question 24: We've read in the Bible how you killed bears and the giant, Goliath. What advice can you give people today in fighting the giants in their lives? 65

Rebecca's Questions 69

Question 25: You had amazing faith in God when you faced Goliath. Why were you so confident? 69

Question 26: When you sinned by killing Bathsheba's husband, did you think that God wasn't watching? 71

Question 27: How did you write the psalms? What was your favorite psalm? 73

Question 28: You played the harp for Saul. What effect did this have on him? 76

Question 29: What was it like to wait all those years, knowing that you were anointed to be king of Israel but not being able to fulfill your destiny? 78

Matthew's Question 80

Question 30: David, what are your final words? 80

I'd love to hear from you 83

How to Sponsor a Book Project 85

Other Books by Matthew Robert Payne 86

About Matthew Robert Payne 89

Matthew's Question

Question 1: How do you feel about being here today, David?

It's a real honor to come down here. I'm excited to be invited here by the Lord Jesus and God the Father to come down and speak to the people on earth. I'm aware that I'm only going to be speaking to a few people, those who are interested in buying this book. Some people will listen to it, and others will recommend it to their friends. It's worth it to me to speak and to come to earth just to speak to the few people who find it and read it.

Heaven is a little different than what you think and how you understand it. On earth, someone's popular when millions of people watch a film and when the movie breaks records at the box office. People consider that the movie is a successful film. Sometimes a film might have a better message with a wider impact on the people that watch it. Other times, it might not be as well-known and might not do as well at the box office. On one hand, millions of people watch this movie that's a box-office success. It might be all flowery and a feel-good movie, but it doesn't necessarily have much of an effect on the people that watch it. A smaller film might have a major impact on people and cause real-life changes to the people that watch it. I ask, "Which is the better film?" Is it the one that was heralded as the great success of the year that made people feel good? Or was it a film that fewer people saw that wasn't a success financially, but the people who watched it came away from it, considering their lives and making changes?

The same is true for this book. Someone like Joyce Meyer, Benny Hinn, or another successful person in Christian circles could have released it so that it was read by hundreds and thousands or even millions of people, depending on the level of success. But if they released it, they might not go into all the details that we will cover in this book. Instead we are releasing this book through you, which will have a limited readership, but you have the freedom to allow me to say some things that might be controversial or might be more honest, real, heart-warming, and challenging than a great leader might say.

We've understood you, Matthew, to be very real. You are becoming very experienced at conveying our words in truth and with the reality that we want to express. This book addresses some difficult subjects, questions, and answers, and some people might not know how to receive these things. Because these words are coming through you, you're quite able to say what you think and not worry about the consequences. Someone popular might have more people read their books, but the popular people wouldn't do an interview with David. Their reputation couldn't handle the negative feedback from speaking to people from heaven.

I'm ecstatic to be here and to speak to you, dear reader. If you are reading or listening to this book, it's for a special reason. The Holy Spirit has a specific purpose for directing you to this book so that I can speak to you. I'm glad to be here.

I walked to the gas station with Matthew and spent a little time with him as he met the gas-station attendant. I saw firsthand how he interacts with strangers and how loving and supportive he is of people who serve him. I've watched from heaven and seen him interact with others. I have watched movies of Matthew living his life, but it was fun to personally be here with him. It's so nice to be in his house and to be a part of this process. I truly enjoy Matthew. I've watched him for years in heaven. He is known in heaven by many of the people there. He is lying down on a couch where he normally does his interviews, and I am speaking comfortably into his recorder.

We actually use this question, not so much for information, but we use it so that Matthew can settle in and get used to the anointing. He relaxes before his first series of questions. You might not have known that about the purpose of this question and why this question is in many of his books. But one of the main reasons for this question is to calm Matthew's nerves like an artist singing or a musician playing. He might be nervous during the first song, but a couple of songs into the concert, the nerves are gone with a pure flow of creativity and talent. The same is true for this interview. Matthew uses this question to relax and put himself in the right frame of mind with a great capacity to carry and convey the words to the people.

Nicola's Questions

Question 2: What were your thoughts when you were dancing before the Ark of the Lord? How did it affect you when Michal despised your dancing?

First and foremost, the day that I brought the Ark of the Covenant, the very symbol of God, the very presence of God, into Jerusalem, the Holy City, was the most enjoyable, the most fantastic, and exciting day of my life. As a worshipper, I wholly loved God. My whole heart was focused on him. My whole purpose for living was to encourage the people of Israel to worship God, follow him, and serve him.

I was so excited to have the Ark of the Covenant come to the capital city, the city of God, and make its home there. I can't express it in words. Some men would say that their wedding day or the birth of their son was the highlight of their lives. Others might say that being awarded an honor in the workplace as the best scientist in the world was their best day. Some men might receive the Nobel Peace Prize and document that as the greatest event in their life. These are all great things, and different men and women have different events that become their favorite. For women, their wedding day would probably be one of their most special days. For some women, the achievements of their son or daughter at university—receiving a bachelor's or master's degree or becoming a doctor—might be the highlight of their lives. We all have our special days. We all have events and special days in our lives that stand out. I was wholly committed to God.

My God was my breath. It would be useless for me to live without knowing God and without having a relationship with him. Remember what happened to Saul when the Holy Spirit departed from him? I witnessed that. It would have been the most spiritually heartbreaking thing that could happen to me. If the Holy Spirit had departed from me, I would have killed myself and ended my life. There is nothing like the presence of God, and that was paramount to me. So it was a special moment when the actual presence of God, the Ark of the Covenant, came into the city. The people of God, the people of Israel, recognized the presence of God. The ark was previously in a different city in another man's house, and great blessings came to his house because of God's presence. It was a tremendous and exciting day and the highlight of my life. I was filled with joy.

In 2 Samuel 6:14, I was dancing without any undergarments. While dancing, I exposed myself, and my wife complained. The daughter of Saul that I had married grumbled and said negative things to me and about me after the fact. Know this: if God truly moves in your life and you have an outstanding achievement or a remarkable event in the spiritual realm or if you powerfully experience the presence of God as a spiritual high, you can bet that Satan will have something to say in opposition.

You can always bet that when something successful or outstanding happens in the spiritual realm, Satan will put his two cents in. In this case, Michal put her two cents in as well. She had things to say about my dancing and the fact that I exposed myself, which hurt me. Even so, her words didn't take away the joy of the memory from me or destroy my fabulous excitement of the event.

From that time on, Michal was barren. (See 2 Samuel 6:23.) God certainly closed her womb and acted on my behalf. Christians today don't really understand that God looks on his anointed ones, and if you strike a hand against someone who is anointed, sometimes God will play his hand and strike a hand against you.

Some people are finding that out. I say it because you are living in these times. Many people have risen up against Donald Trump, who is the Lord's anointed, and they've ended up the worse for the wear because they raised a hand against Donald. This was true with me as Michal suffered and was barren from that point on. This was a real embarrassment and shameful for her as a woman at that time.

But nothing took away my joy. I still remember that memory clearly as I speak of it; it's still a highlight of my life.

Question 3: How did you feel about the trouble with your sons, especially Absalom and Amnon? What would you have done differently in how you handled them?

At the risk of stating the obvious, I want to say that rape is never good. A woman should never be raped. This is never an excuse. I personally raped Bathsheba and had my way with her without her permission. It seems like the sins of the father were passed down to my children. When I heard the news, it was like a stab in the heart and caused me further suffering.

I lost my first child with Bathsheba due to my sin. God took the child. Even so, punishment still seemed to come through my sons. I truly loved Tamar, and she was shattered. *Shattered* is a strong word to describe how she felt when Amnon raped her. Absalom was furious and couldn't hide his rage.

I definitely admire a person who doesn't hide their feelings. In the world today, people often walk around with masks on to hide their feelings. Many Christians are secretly unhappy with God and hold resentment in their heart toward him. They might resent him because they haven't been promoted or because they are sick or because they don't have the opportunities that other people have had. People today walk around with all these resentments toward God and toward other people. And yet even with the resentments toward others, they wear a mask when they meet and greet the person with smiles, love, laughter, and hugs. Inwardly, they'd like to rip the person apart, and they want the person to suffer. Outwardly, they are all smiles and affection.

Absalom wasn't like that. His whole personality changed; he was very angry. I tried to talk to him and console him. But he was so full of rage that he later plotted to kill Amnon.

God has given men free will. We wish we could change many things that happen while living on earth. Many people suffer because of free will. God can't come down from heaven and stop every abuser from abusing. If God stopped every abuser, earth would never function properly. There would be continual disruptions, which would make it a very strange universe. People have a free will. And as a father, I was like God; I could only have said so much to Absalom. Now that I live in heaven with greater understanding and wisdom, I can say quite honestly that I could not have done anything as a man. Even if I were God, I couldn't have changed Absalom's heart. He burned with rage and anger, which was plain to see.

You know, in life, you commonly have regrets. People can have regrets about situations that happen. I could continue to question myself and say that I should have spoken to Absalom one more time, and perhaps if I had one more conversation with him, it would have stopped him. But it's important to live a life free from regrets and even with no regrets if possible. Part of the wonderment of living with God is that you can confess your sins and be freed from guilt and condemnation through the Spirit of God, which was what I did that in that situation.

I was so upset when Absalom turned on me. I was afraid for my life and ran and hid until matters were resolved. Once again, this was the fallout from my sin, a punishment for when I took Bathsheba as my wife. Once again, I seemed to suffer for my decision. I truly loved Absalom. In one way, it was very courageous of him to supplant me.

Interestingly, I always thought the best of people. You'll learn this about me as we progress through the interview. I had this childlike heart and faith. I didn't see the bad in people but only ever saw the good in them. I tended to ignore or look past their faults. And so I saw the strengths in Absalom: his leadership qualities, his desire to be king, and his desire to rule and reign. Even in the midst of running and hiding from the threat, I still admired him. That might be strange for someone who thinks the worst of others or who naturally sees what's wrong with people. But I always saw the best in others.

Would I change things? I don't think I could have done anything differently. Once again, I'll reiterate that I didn't have any regrets at the end of my life. All my regrets, missteps, wrongdoings, and shortcomings were eradicated, forgiven, and given to God. They have all been dealt with. I encourage you all to live life so that you are not carried away by your mistakes and missteps. Keep an open conscience toward God and deal with past mistakes so that you aren't weighed down by regrets.

Question 4: After you succeeded in life and had so much victory in battles, what was it like to deal with Saul's jealousy of you?

I was saying in the last question that I had a pure heart. Before God, I had a childlike faith with this innocence about me. This is different for many people. Some people might think it strange to consider that you could live a life where you dealt with people, including their faults and all kinds of situations and experiences, yet you still loved them no matter what.

You have a much different perspective when you don't look at the bad in others or dwell on misfortune and the misguided and terrible parts of people. Even when you meet terrible people, you can learn to focus on the good parts of them.

Matthew once dealt with the doorman and security personnel of a striptease place where prostitutes and strippers worked. The doorman and employees there were evil as Matthew even saw them use an electric cattle prodder on some of the prostitutes. The prostitutes fell asleep because of their heroin addiction, and these men used the cattle prodder to electrocute them with a jolt to make them go back to work. The prostitutes were heroin addicts who all lived on the premises, and they were trapped there and treated harshly.

Matthew had misgivings about the staff there and wished he could change the situation. He was in there ministering to the prostitutes each night. But Matthew found solace in understanding the staff, knowing that they were family men with their own children. They had their own lives and only did this type of work for finances and to make a living. Matthew found a way to relate to the doorman and security guards through their humanity. They weren't being evil just for the sake of being evil but as a means to an end.

I dealt with Saul in the same way. He was like a father to me, which was his strong point. I came into his palace at a young age and developed a kinship with him. He initially honored and loved me and treated me with respect, giving me a favored position in his household at the palace. I had a love for Saul, and as I started to win battles, I thought that I could serve God and serve the kingdom that Saul ran. I didn't feel that I was doing anything wrong by winning battles and being successful.

I was a very strong fighter, very brave. I was tireless in my fitness levels and the way that I trained and worked out, like you'd say today. I exercised my muscles and built myself up. I was very skilled in warfare. I thought that I should fight on behalf of the country and go to war and excel in battle. I had many face-to-face battles with my mighty men and with the army of Israel. We had tremendous success, and I was very proud and happy with myself. I was quite surprised when Saul rose up in jealousy as the people's hearts started to turn toward me.

The people of God recognized the anointing on my life and that I was a strong fighter. They said that I was a more exceptional fighter than Saul, and Saul became jealous. What can you do if a person is jealous? I tried to be nice to him and to comfort him. I tried to explain away my victories and minimize my successes. I tried to console him and say that, since he was busy running the palace, he didn't have time to be at war or maintain his fitness level. I explained that he didn't have the support of the fighting men that I had. I tried to reason with him and share that it was more of my skill and my ability that was winning the fights and making me so popular. I said that perhaps he wasn't as skilled as I was at fighting. I tried different ways to be at peace with him, but I couldn't console him. Envy and jealousy are very powerful forces. You remember that Cain slew Abel when he was envious and jealous of him. It's a very powerful motivator.

In some ways, Absalom was jealous of me, which was the motivating force behind his desire to become king. Some people are jealous of others in business today in your world, and jealousy drives them to success. Jealousy in a person is very hard to counteract. I tried everything I could. Like I said, I was a pure soul, a pure-hearted person. I saw the best in people. I knew Saul was a great king. I greatly admired him and loved him like a father. You have to remember, I left my father's house when I was very young, and I needed a father figure. Saul was like that to me, and I had nothing but admiration for him. But nothing I could do or say could console him and make up for his jealousy.

Question 5: Why did you have so much love for those who did you wrong, including Saul and others, despite how they treated you?

We have covered some of this in previous questions, but I'll address this further and unpack it a little more. Every one of us who live, every one of us who are born, are given different hearts, mindsets, skills, and abilities. We all are essentially born pure—with a good and innocent heart. Then life seems to happen to us. Some of us are abused sexually; some of us are treated violently; some of us have a missing father; some of us have mothers that are too overbearing.

Different things happen to people that carve away at their character. Well, despite leaving my family and my father's house at such a young age and being taken up by Saul, I had a God-conscious yearning in my heart. I turned out pretty well. I was able to keep purity in my heart no matter what happened. I had a heart like Jesus, a beautiful, loving heart. I suppose the best way to explain what I was like is that I had a personality similar to the personality of Jesus Christ while he was on earth. I was full of love, compassion, kindness, and goodness.

Even when Solomon told God that he wanted wisdom to be able to rule the people—the wisdom of God to make decisions—Solomon actually received his request and desire from the example he'd seen in my life. I ruled my kingdom with wisdom. I had a lot of love and compassion, and Solomon saw that in me. He wanted to model that to the people of God when he ruled.

I had this amazing heart. It's said that I was a man after God's own heart with this heart that only saw good. I certainly had negative experiences. I experienced Saul's envy and jealousy. He chased me for many years and hunted me down. But you know this—in the cave, when he went to relieve himself, and I had a chance to kill him, I took a piece of his clothing to prove that I was there. (See 1 Samuel 24:11.) I didn't turn my hand against the Lord's anointed. Part of the reason that I didn't kill Saul was because I loved him. Scripture says in 1 Peter 4:8, "Love covers a multitude of sins." Nothing that Saul could have done against me or to me would have stopped my love for him.

Sometimes, you see a father treating his child violently, and yet the child still loves his father and still respects him. In some ways, like I said, Saul was a father figure to me. I still loved him. I still have love in my heart for him.

In this world, so many men are broken. They have flaws and are less than perfect. So many fathers are alcoholics and physically, spiritually, and sexually abusing their children or wives. They are just broken men that need counseling and healing. These men do so much harm in this world. Saul was one of them, someone who couldn't handle the responsibility of being a king. They say that power corrupts, and it certainly corrupted Saul.

I understood that he was broken, but I loved his strong points. I loved different aspects of his personality that aren't fleshed out well or talked about much in the Bible. People don't understand him as a man. The Bible seems to emphasize his bad faults and what he did wrong. But he was chosen by God, and we have to consider that first of all. People tend to forget that God chose him. People today look at him in a negative light and only see the wrong that he did. But he had a lot of positive qualities, and I truly loved him. And I still love him. I have such fond memories of the time before I started winning wars, before I became such a success, before he turned on me and became jealous of me. I have so many wonderful memories of spending time with him, fighting with him, practicing swordsmanship with him, practicing with his army, being trained by him, mentored by him, and raised by him. My pure heart, my selfless, loving, Christlike heart, allowed me to have people in my life that acted against me while I still remained pure and in a position of grace and love toward everyone.

Question 6: Ziklag was destroyed by fire, and your men's wives and children were stolen. When you and your men came to Ziklag, the men were talking of stoning you. The Bible says that you "found strength in the Lord" (1 Samuel 30:6). What did God say to you at that time, and how did you encourage yourself?

My men were furious that their wives and children were taken. To truly appreciate this story, you need to put yourself in the other person's shoes. In order to resolve a conflict between you and another person, you should take the time to focus on how the other person is feeling. If what happened to the other person had happened to you, how would you feel and how would you react?

I was trying to resolve the situation, so I put myself in their shoes. They wanted to stone me, and I didn't mind dying. I loved God and had a heart that was yearning to be face to face with him. But I also had a mission to serve him and his people. I knew that it was my job to be king and to rule. God had a purpose for my life, and I wasn't ready to lay it down at that moment because I knew that it wasn't his will.

So the first thing that I did was petition God for the men and for their hearts to bring them understanding and comfort. I knew how they felt as my wife and children had been taken as well. I spent some time asking God to touch them, change their hearts, and help them see that we could solve this and recover our women and children. Then I worshipped the Lord. "As for me and my house, we will serve the Lord," Joshua said in Joshua 24:15. I was between a rock and a hard place, to use one of your clichés!

I had a strong relationship with God, and I knew that God had the solution to this. When you are given no other option, when you're put in a place where you're cornered with your back against the wall, when your only help can come from the Lord, when you've had a life filled with harassment, trials, and terrors, it quickly becomes your second nature to run to God. If I modelled anything in the psalms that I wrote, if they had a theme, it's this: When all else fails, turn to God and submit to him and plead your case with him. Run to God for your solution. I did that and then wept.

After I wept, I worshipped God and told him that if this was the end, I looked forward to seeing him and that I loved him and thanked him for allowing me to be on earth. Even so, I asked him to please comfort me and give me an answer and a solution. God said that he would play out his hand with me, and he would deliver me. He said that he was very happy with me, that once again when all else was failing, I had turned to him. God made it very plain to me that he chose my heart above all others and that he was very pleased with me and that he loved me. He assured me that he'd get me out of this fix, and then God sang along with my worship.

Have you ever experienced it, reader, where you sense that God or his angels were singing along as you worshipped? Have you ever considered that you could sing and worship the Father, and the Father would sing along with you? As I worshipped God and gave him a new song, the Father sang with me, which was so encouraging. It was a precious moment. I have difficulty in conveying how special it was. It was truly remarkable to hear God sing, to hear him in my spirit, singing along with me. It was this special moment for us to connect. God proved time and time again that he was there for me.

As you read this, and as you live your life on earth, I want to assure you that God is dependable despite your previous experience with God, with Christians, with the Christian faith, or with life. He is loyal, loving, and a refuge. Misconceptions and lies from the enemy stop you from believing his goodness. If you make a practice of running to God even in the midst of trouble, you'll find that he has a beautiful temperament and personality, and he'll prove himself faithful toward you. He'll prove himself a deliverer. Many times, he delivered our armies and brought us success. Many times, he delivered me personally when I was in a fix, and this time with him was no different.

Question 7: You are the famous writer of the Psalms, which are still being put to music today. What would you say to Christian songwriters of our day?

I'm going to tell you, Nicola, that I certainly appreciate your questions today. All of your questions have been amazing, and they've stretched Matthew a lot. I have enjoyed speaking so far and answering your questions. What would I say to songwriters today? Matthew heard the Lord say this to a songwriter about ten years ago. And I'll repeat it because God said it, and no one can triumph over God.

He told the songwriter not to focus on the audience or on the many, on whether your song will become a hit, but to focus on the one person hearing your song who is totally transformed. My advice to songwriters is to focus on touching and changing a heart. When you write a song, take away the worry about it becoming popular and forget about the pressure of writing something that many people would like. Instead reach into yourself and touch the heart of a person. Write a song. It doesn't matter if thousands of people hear it. If one individual hears it and it totally transforms their lives, it's worth it. Focus on that one person rather than focusing on touching everybody's heart. Focus on touching one individual's heart.

The same is true for what I'm saying today. I'm focused on you, the reader. You are reading this book, and I'm sharing my message for you. It's not for hundreds or thousands of people. The mere fact that I've come from heaven and that I'm in Matthew, possessing and speaking through him at the moment, is for you. The mere fact that we're even writing this book means that we want to touch a heart, and it doesn't matter that this book doesn't touch millions of hearts. We want to touch your heart.

Secondly, I would say to a songwriter, write a song that's going to touch the very heart of God. Some songs will touch individuals, and some songs touch the heart of God. It wasn't hard for me, but there's a lot of pressure today to be popular with all the hits and with every album that needs a single or a hit. I'd imagine that every worship band needs to have songs that churches adopt and sing. Christian musicians or any musicians face so much pressure to write a popular hit. Try and touch God's heart.

Think about how you would act if you were alone and face to face with God and if you walked into the throne room and if everyone left and it was just you underneath the throne of God, at the bottom of two hundred stairs. If you were standing there and an orchestra came and played the music, what song would you sing to God? How would you make God cry? What would you sing to him to bring tears to his eyes? How would you touch the very heart of God? Think about that! Take away the pressure to write a good song that will impress people. Instead think about the lyrics. Think of the music and the lyrics that will touch the very heart of God.

Another aspect to focus on is not to think about your song becoming a hit on earth but focus on writing a song that will become a hit in heaven. In *Michael Jackson Speaks from Heaven*, a book of Matthew's, he explained that heaven holds weekly competitions for the best song of the week with a contemporary chart and a worship chart. Michael told Matthew that he'd won the "Best Song of the Week" for the worship song. Instead focus on winning what might be the "Best Song of the Week" in heaven, and focus on writing a song that the people of heaven will truly love and love to worship with. Focus on writing a song that will touch an individual's heart and that will touch the heart of God.

I realize that you've brought out the worship leader and the songwriter in me. Matthew's not sure how the best songwriters of the world would judge what I've just said. But it's solid advice. In my glorified state, I can't offer any better advice. The best thing I can do is offer this explanation. You know, Michael Jackson used to write a hundred songs for every album that he wrote. He only chose fifteen songs out of a hundred songs that he'd write. Another lesson that I can tell you is to not just write one song but write many, and in the practice of writing many, you'll come across a song from time to time that will stand out from the rest.

These three points in practice follow:

- Write a song that is focused on touching an individual,
- Write a song that's focused on touching God, and
- Write a song that the people of heaven will be glad to worship to.

If you can coordinate those three and align them in one song, then you will have a wonderful song. So thank you, Nicola, for the question. I truly enjoyed bringing out my worship side to the people of God.

Question 8: What do you have to say about your friendship and love for Jonathan and his crippled son, Mephibosheth?

First of all, I want to say that some commentators have suggested that I had a codependent and unhealthy relationship with Jonathan. Matthew has heard some liberal commentators say that we had a homosexual relationship. Liberals will be liberals, and theologians will be theologians. I do want to dismiss those rumors. If you've heard that I had a codependent or homosexual relationship with Jonathan, I want to totally put a stop to that rumor. That was not and is not the case. Many theologians and commentators will be strictly judged if they even make it to heaven.

Jonathan was the epitome of a brother, a friend, and even closer than a brother. Scripture says in 1 Samuel 18:1 that Jonathan was so close to me that our souls were knit together. Just as I mentioned that Saul was like a father, Jonathan was like my brother. I was removed from my family at a young age and got to know Jonathan. I also married his sister, Michal, which made him my brother-in-law. I truly loved him. How can you put such a special friendship into words?

In America, you have a peanut-butter-and-jelly sandwich. How can you have peanut butter without jelly? They go together, and they're made for each other. In Australia, Matthew has a pavlova with ice cream. You can have pavlova without ice cream, but a pavlova and ice cream go together.

So too, we were made to know each other. Jonathan was God's provision for me, and God knew that I needed a friend. At one stage, Jonathan even informed me if I was in trouble with his father, Saul. Jonathan acted as my spy. He also realized that I was going to succeed Saul as king and that he wasn't going to be king himself but that I'd been anointed as king. He wasn't jealous or afraid of me. He knew that I loved him.

I became king after Saul and Jonathan died in battle. I later found his son, who was crippled, and I saw that his son was afraid because in those times, a conquering king would wipe out the family of the former king and leave no relative alive. So he was scared. But I brought him into the palace and reassured him and gave him a seat at my dining table.

Furthermore, a king did not usually make it a practice to have someone crippled or maimed at the table. But I broke that tradition and had a crippled boy, a crippled man, at my table. He grew up to be a man and to love me so much as a father. That is like a symbol to everyone that God accepts the unclean; God accepts the crippled; God accepts you despite what's wrong with you. You could be an adulterer, a pedophile, a child abuser, or someone who struggles with any sort of sin, and God will have you.

Do you know that if Hitler had repented as the armies came for him, if he would have cried out to God for forgiveness, God would have accepted him? God accepts everybody. The shed blood of Jesus is enough sacrifice to cleanse anybody.

I went against the accepted practice in two ways. First, I had Jonathan's son at my table. Second, I did not kill him even though he was part of the former king's family but saved his life. In these ways, I was a forerunner of Christ who did many things differently from the accepted practice. He treated women differently, treated his enemies differently, and treated sinners differently. I was a radical forerunner of Jesus Christ.

I loved Jonathan. His son came to realize how much I loved his father through the time that we spent together. The son is in heaven with us now, a grown man who runs around. He is not crippled anymore. It's a message to you that, no matter how you're suffering on earth and whether or not you are ever healed on earth through a miracle, you can be sure that you'll be free from that suffering and free from the way that you're dealing with life in heaven. You will enjoy total freedom and a new life there.

So we come to the conclusion of Nicola's questions, and once again, I want to say to Nicola, I'm very happy with your questions. It was a real pleasure to answer them. Matthew's found an easier way to do his interviews by asking his close friends to come up with questions. I've finished your questions, and I hope you enjoyed my answers.

Mary's Questions

Question 9: Can you describe what it felt like to be called a man after God's own heart?

It was very humbling. How would you feel if you were given the Nobel Peace Prize? How would you feel if you were voted the most loving father of a country? How would you feel if you were told by God that you're his favorite person in the world? Many people would say that God doesn't have favorites as the Bible says in Acts 10:34 that "God is no respecter of persons." People assume that God loves everyone equally, and yet God has levels of favor for people.

He has a special place in his heart for some people. In scripture, God boasts about the type of person and the type of king that I was. I had a special place in his heart.

It is incredibly humbling to be called a man after God's own heart. He told me that he loves me and that he loves my heart and that I was a man after his own heart. It was recorded in the Bible, and I read it after I came to heaven. Sometimes, you're completely shocked and amazed by something that's said about you. In other words, it definitely humbles you.

I can understand why this was said about me. I was a forerunner of Jesus Christ and a shadow of what was to come. I had this remarkably pure heart. When you read scripture and the stories of my life, you're aware that I went through a lot. If you read the Psalms, you'll realize how much I suffered. Many people came after me. My life was marked in many ways for suffering and trial. Yet I remained pure throughout. This purity is like a heart that's wholly devoted to God and that fully seeks after him.

Matthew thought more about what it means to be a man after God's own heart, which is worth putting in here. A man after God's own heart has two main meanings—two ways that you can understand it. The first meaning is a man who is pursuing God's heart, a man after God's own heart who wants to do everything he can to please God and make him happy. That's one understanding.

Another understanding with a similar meaning is a man who wants God's heart on things, a man who is after the heart of God to operate in his love. An example is Solomon who wanted a heart of wisdom to be able to judge the people and treat them fairly. That was one aspect of being a man after the heart of God; he could act wisely.

As a reader of this book, you might be attacked, and people might come against you. You might have many opportunities to become envious, angry, and bitter. You might be tempted to let these negative experiences change your heart from pure to corrupted, dirty, foul, and stained. Many persistent and thorough assaults come after people to harden their hearts. These assaults are launched to actually change the heart's structure. Satan often succeeds in corrupting a person's heart, and many people who deal with this need healing and restoration.

No matter what came against me, I was able to keep my pure heart. Acts 13:22 recorded that I had a special heart and that I was a man after God's own heart. I'm held up as a symbol of what's right and what's possible. All of my psalms help convey the kind of person that I was—loving, accepting, beautiful—and who I currently am in heaven. Of course, your character improves and is a whole lot better in heaven. Thank you for your question, Mary. I look forward to going through each of your questions and answering them with all of my love, attention, and adoration.

Question 10: What advice would you give to someone who has committed adultery or who is thinking about committing adultery? Or someone who's currently committing adultery?

Adultery is very harmful although it's an acceptable practice in today's society. All kinds of sins are acceptable today, including homosexuality. You can actually get in trouble if you say that homosexuality is not a normal way of life. Sleeping with prostitutes has always been an accepted part of society. Perhaps people frown on it, but some people believe that it's better for a man to sleep with prostitutes than to commit rape. A time is even coming when it will be acceptable to sleep with dummies and robots. Life on earth is becoming very difficult.

A common cliché states, "The grass is always greener on the other side of the fence." So many times, people commit adultery. But people might not start out with the desire to commit adultery. They don't say, "Well, I'm married, but I want to sleep with my secretary. I hired her so that I can seduce her and she can become my lover." Affairs might begin with someone not feeling appreciated at home and then developing a friendship with someone of the opposite sex that becomes more loving and understanding. When a man meets a woman who is giving him positive encouragement and life-affirming words and when he loves other qualities about her, she can become attractive to him.

There are often two sides to adultery. Many times, when there's a lack in her husband or in her current partner, a woman might seek attention from another man or find his attention appealing. The same holds true for a man who looks for attention from someone besides his wife. Sometimes, he's not happy with something about his wife. We can play the blame game and say that it's never the right thing to do under any circumstances. Adultery is certainly condemned in the Bible. One of the Ten Commandments is that you shouldn't commit adultery. It's not right, and I do not approve of it at all, but I am certainly guilty of it. I committed adultery when I raped Bathsheba. It's a heartbreaking situation.

Many children are the result of adulterous affairs. If you're not happy with your wife or your husband, God doesn't approve of divorce as a solution. You should not start looking elsewhere for a new relationship if you're not happy with your current spouse. But people are people. Many people can't handle being single or alone. They start a relationship with another partner before they leave the relationship they're in.

Many people rebound from one relationship to the next. God doesn't approve of this. He doesn't want his creation to commit spiritual adultery by having any other gods but him, and he doesn't want you to put anything between him and you or serve money, a job, or another person. But people commit spiritual adultery against God all the time, and so the practice of having other lovers will hurt you, and I fully recommend that you don't do it. But even in my redeemed state in glory, I still have to be honest with you. That's what I did, so it's almost hypocritical of me to speak on the subject. I had a beautiful wife and a beautiful son. I truly loved Bathsheba, and I can't imagine my life without her. Even Jesus was descended from Bathsheba.

My message is that God can make something good from anything. While no one should commit fornication, many people do it. Men shouldn't sleep with other men, but they still do it. People shouldn't cheat on tests, but many people do. Telling people that they can't sin isn't the answer because it just doesn't work. When you're told not to do something, you actually do it more frequently. (See Romans 5:20.) If people see a sign to not touch the wet paint, they will touch the wet paint anyhow to check if it's still wet. A command actually increases the likelihood that people will do what is commanded against. I advise you not to go down the road of adultery or fornication. But know that I love you, and God loves you, and he's a redeeming God.

Question 11: What chapter in the book of Psalms encouraged you the most?

My favorite Psalm is the favorite of the world too. The most popular psalm is Psalm 23. "The Lord is my shepherd; I shall not want." This encouraging psalm speaks to my relationship with God. It's a very comforting chapter that encourages many people with the words that it contains. I had a close relationship with God on earth, and I was never in want. "The Lord is my shepherd; I shall not want." I was never in want. He used to take me and make me lie down in green pastures. He comforted me and showed me places of rest. With all my trials and stresses, he was able to comfort and restore my soul. He was able to bring me solace, comfort, and love. He was a loving God, and I had a real love affair with him.

Matthew tends to see my life as full of struggle, trouble, and anxiety with stresses on every side. Matthew doesn't often read the Psalms because he finds them depressing, and he doesn't know the

Psalms that are encouraging. He doesn't like to read that part of the Bible because, so often, it's depressing and sad. I don't know if you feel the same way as a reader. Do you find comfort in the Psalms, or do you think that they are distressing and discouraging like Matthew does?

"Yea, though I walk through the valley of the shadow of death, I will fear no evil; for You are with me" (verse 4a). Many times, my life was at stake. People came against me, surrounded me, and tried to take me out. I was always comforted by the Lord and brought to a place of refreshing with him. The Lord was my strength, my shield, and he was my father. He was able to encourage me, be with me, and give me peace and comfort. He corrected me; he guided me! "Your rod and staff, they comfort me" (verse 4 b). He was able to bring direction to me through his love and was able to discipline me through various means.

"You prepare a table before me in the presence of my enemies" (verse 5a). I saw that happen. "You anoint my head with oil; My cup runs over. Surely goodness and mercy shall follow me all the days of my life; and I will dwell in the house of the Lord forever" (verse 5b–6). I am now dwelling in the house of the Lord, and I'm very comforted by my relationship with God. I'm in a very happy place in heaven. I'm celebrated and loved here. Everyone in heaven knows who I am and celebrates me.

So many people in heaven knew of me, knew of the Bible. Many people in heaven had read the Bible, had read of my exploits. Even people in heaven that lived before me knew who I was and had seen my life on the screens in heaven.

Heaven has screens where you can look at a person's life and history and see the future. When I say screens in heaven, you can understand what that means if you don't regularly read Matthew's books. Anyone can look at a saint's life or watch a movie of their whole life in about two hours of earth time. You can watch a person's whole existence and see everything they've been through.

I went through a lot, and Psalm 23 captures the essence of my life. Of course, if we met face to face, Mary, and you opened your Bible and I was able to speak with you, we'd be able to turn from psalm to psalm, and I could answer your questions.

Also, Rebecca, you asked another question that wasn't included in this book: "What's your favorite psalm?" Psalm 23 is my favorite psalm. But, Rebecca, I could sit down with you or with Mary and Nicola and share some of my favorite psalms face to face. You could share some of your favorite psalms with me. I could talk about them in depth.

Readers, you only have to accept that I want to come into your house. You can sense my presence in your house, and you can ask me questions through the spirit like you speak to God. You could ask me through the spirit what I think of certain psalms, and you could have a discussion with me. I encourage you all to ask me to come to your house and let me speak with you face to face and share some of the highlights of your favorite psalms with you.

Question 12: When you realized God was not going to allow you to build the temple but that it would be built by your son Solomon, how did you feel about that?

I want to tell you, Mary, that this was a very good question for you to ask. Many people would ask this same question if given the opportunity. Your next question is, "What one thing in your life did you regret the most?" It's a toss-up between when I committed adultery with Bathsheba and not being able to build the temple.

But I have to choose what cut me to the core the most, so I'll combine this question with the next question.

The thing that cut me to the heart the most was not being able to build a temple. Remember when I said that I was shattered when Tamar was raped by her brother. I was also shattered when God told me that I couldn't build a temple. It might be easier to understand if you compare it to a worshipper who had his voice taken from him. Imagine a world-renowned worship singer with a worship band who had a throat infection that caused him to permanently lose his voice. If you're a worshipper who can no longer sing, grief would overshadow your life from that point on. It would almost be unbearable to sit in church with people worshipping if you could not join in and would continually break your heart. It shattered me when God told me that I couldn't build a temple and hurt me deeply.

Of course, I serve a God who knows all things: our past, our values, and our futures. He only wants the best for us. A lie of the enemy says that God withholds things from us and that he isn't fair. God had his reasons, but I was shattered and cut to the heart that I couldn't build a temple. But what did I do? As a worshipper, you have to remember that I was the king of worship. How was I going to progress? Was I going to let that forever mark me and live in depression for the rest of my life like the worshipper who lost his voice that I mentioned? Or was I going to clean myself up, shave, anoint my head with oil, and be refreshed?

I lost a son—my first-born son to Bathsheba! I moaned, and I cried, and I pleaded with God. When he actually died, I then washed myself, cleaned myself up, and came out fresh again. I said, "God knows best!" Then I had to come to a point where I put away my moaning. I put away my sorrow, and I praised God for the God that he is. He is a wonderful, beautiful, loving, all-knowing, all-wise God.

You can either let setbacks cause bitterness, anger, and strife in your life, or you can confess your sins—your concerns, worries, hardships, troubles, and struggles to God, and you can move on and get over them. God helped me accept the fact that Solomon was going to build the temple as I used the remainder of my life to collect and furnish the materials that would build the temple for Solomon. In this way, I used my wealth and my influence with the people and partly financed the materials for the temple, and I was pleased to play a role in it.

Here is a lesson for you, reader. You can have a setback. Negative events might deeply hurt and affect you, but you can choose to get over them. This is a choice. Do you let that affect you for the rest of your life, or do you confess your heart attitude, your struggle, and your disappointment with God, and move on and turn over a new page in your book and open a new chapter to your life? How do you handle it?

For many of you reading or listening to this book, you haven't forgotten the painful things that have happened to you. Some of you haven't dealt with them, resulting in envy, bitterness, and pain toward people that you haven't forgiven and even toward God for allowing it to happen. You need to learn how to move on. You need to learn how to cope and how to live life every day, enjoying a new day to be invigorated with the glory of God and refreshed in his presence. You can live each day and live your life with no regrets. That's how I want to close this chapter.

I kept short accounts with God. So when Nathan corrected me and spoke to me about the man with a lot of sheep who took another man's sheep who owned only one sheep, I was cut to the heart and corrected by God. Of course, people would look at my life and think that the biggest regret was when I committed adultery with Bathsheba. Yes, it was terrible, but a great son, Solomon, came from that union. You also have to consider how deeply I loved Bathsheba. She was a real favorite of mine as a wife. So it's important, dear reader, for you to live a life with no regrets, to live a life where you're happy with your decisions. You might not be happy with how everything happens, but you need to take everything before God, submit it to him, and live a life with a fresh conscience and outlook every single day. On your deathbed, don't have any regrets!

Question 13: Can you describe the happiest moment of your life?

This takes us back to a former question. The happiest day of my life was when the Ark of the Covenant came into Jerusalem. I was so jubilant, especially considering my position as a king and a prophet. In the Old Testament, I could hear God speak and understood his anointing and his presence and, in greater measure, the presence of God that accompanied the Ark of the Covenant. The happiest day of my life was when the tabernacle was set up so that I could go and offer sacrifices and worship in the tabernacle in Jerusalem.

As a reader, you might not understand this. As a worshipper, everything in your life is focused on God. It was so amazing to be able to bring the presence of God into my capital city, into my life, and into my people's lives so that they could go into the tabernacle and worship and feel the tangible presence of God in their midst. As the leader of Israel with God dwelling in our midst, this allowed other people to feel what I felt with the presence of God in my life. I was jubilant and filled with ecstasy!

You have a drug called Ecstasy. People take it to feel this jubilant, excited mood and to be transported to a place of joy. That's how I felt on that day. I remember that day. I was so proud.

I must say that I was so pleased and proud of the day that Donald Trump went and kissed the Wailing Wall. Another day that pleased me was when Donald Trump announced that he would move his government embassy to Jerusalem and make Jerusalem the capital of Israel. I was so overjoyed in heaven. The whole of heaven was interested. Jerusalem is the eternal capital of Israel, and mankind on earth should recognize this. So we were thrilled the day that Donald announced that. Donald Trump makes us very happy; he is a man after God's own heart. He is a bit of a scoundrel, and he rubs people the wrong way. He uses salty language, and he's rough around the edges, and yet we love him in heaven.

This was such an exciting time for me as I brought the Ark of the Covenant home to Jerusalem and set up the tabernacle there in a tent.

Of course, I enjoyed the day I was married to Bathsheba. I truly loved her. I was overjoyed on the day that we gave birth to Solomon. As Solomon grew, a mark of favor was on his life. Solomon had supernatural wisdom and was an amazing boy. Normally, a king's son is tutored by servants and the wise men of the kingdom: the prophets and the philosophers. Custom dictated that the people full of wisdom tutored a king's son, especially one that was marked to be the king. But Solomon was like twelve-year-old Jesus in the temple when he amazed the teachers of the law; he used to amaze his teachers with his wisdom. Long before Solomon asked for the wisdom of God, he already possessed supernatural wisdom. Solomon made me so proud and happy. Of course, part of the reason for this was because he was the son of Bathsheba, the love of my life. Jesus descended from me and from Bathsheba and Solomon. He's in heaven; he was a great king, and he served the Lord incredibly well. There was no fighting while he was king. The Lord God truly honored him. As a father, he brought me much honor and glory.

I'll also say that Trump's children shine forth the character of their father. His children bring him glory as they are well-mannered and beautiful. We're extremely proud of him as a leader and proud of his children. Wouldn't it be great if one of his children became president too?

Question 14: What advice do you have for Christians in 2018 who are trying to live for the Lord but who are being attacked by the enemy?

A cliché says, "Whatever doesn't kill you makes you stronger." I could answer this question with that cliché and leave it at that. Concentrate on the meaning of that cliché as the answer. But I'll spend some time unpacking this further as I have some other comments to add.

First of all, I want to clarify that God sees what happens in your life, but he isn't always responsible for what happens in your life. Mankind has free will and acts accordingly. Many children are sexually abused and violently treated. Many children are sold into slavery by their parents. Many young people are lured away by child traffickers, traffickers who promised them a good job in America. They come to America, and their passports are taken, and they are forced into some type of slavery, sexual or otherwise. Many terrible things happen in this world because of man's free will, man's ability to do evil things. One of the biggest misconceptions in the world, especially for Christians, is that God is in control.

When you preach to people and share that God is in control, they are doubly hurt because they think that God allowed injustices to happen to them. "God is in control, so he must want me to be trafficked. He must want me to be a slave; he must want me to be abused. He must approve of my dad raping me." And that's like a double whammy of suffering—not only suffering because of injustice, man's free will, and evil but also coming to grips with the false belief that God allowed it. Part of understanding suffering and part of getting free from the effects of Satan in this world is realizing that God isn't in control of everything.

God doesn't approve of everything. God doesn't design for you to suffer. God's will is not for you to be hurt. I want to emphasize that to all of you. Now you all might not have been raped, sexually abused, have had a violent father, or have suffered terribly in your life. It's wonderful if you haven't. But for people who have been hurt in serious ways, I want to share with you that God loves you, and he didn't want or plan for that to happen.

With that said, if you have suffered, there's a place in God that you can reach with him if you pursue him. He can help you heal from your wounds, become whole, and help you recover from the injustices that happened to you. The world is a big place. Many opportunities exist for you to discover why you're here and discover what's planned for your life. You can train yourself through many outlets. You can read many books. Matthew has a book called *Finding Your Purpose in Christ*, and you can read that book and go on a path of discovery of why you're here. I strongly suggest that Christians come to understand one thing: as Matthew regularly promotes, they need to understand why they're here.

Another suggestion is to pursue Jesus and learn to reach a place of intimacy with him. Matthew has a book, *7 Keys to Intimacy with Jesus*. We certainly encourage you to read that book and not only to read it but to put it into practice. Practice the seven keys. Walk through the steps and put them into practice in your life. Take the time and make the effort to develop an intimate relationship with Jesus because he is the one that holds the keys for you. He holds your life in his hands. He can direct and sustain you. He has the answers to your life. He has the understanding, and his blood can heal you. He has the power to transform your life. Draw close to him, and pursue him with all of your heart so that you can become his close and intimate friend.

In this way, your life will blossom and will become full and will grow to become everything that you were made to be, and you can be a living light and a real example of love and compassion to the world. So if you've suffered, your very suffering, your very scars, the very things you've been through, can be used to help others who are currently suffering or who have suffered. When you've been through hardship, you can take the experience of that hardship and touch people's lives and encourage them with the lessons that you learned. Find out why you're here, and pursue Jesus and develop an intimate relationship with him.

Question 15: Can you describe the pride you feel in knowing that Jesus referred to you as the son of David in the Bible?

Jesus was referred to as the son of David, and it is very humbling to be called by the same term. Once again, it's similar to being called a man after God's own heart. The following honored and amazed me: that Jesus was descended from me and that he was officially called the Son of David.

I've watched all the footage of Jesus's life on the screens of heaven. Everyone in heaven has had the opportunity to watch the whole life of Jesus from his birth to his resurrection and ascension. They've watched and heard everything that Jesus had to say and everything that he experienced, including everything that wasn't even recorded in the Bible as John explains in John 21:25. People in heaven understand all of Jesus's teachings and parables, everything that he taught and ever did, and how he healed everyone.

It's so amazing that Jesus was called the Son of David. It fills me with so much pride, not pride in a bad way that puffs up people. This pride makes me so happy. I'm known as David in heaven. People know that Jesus was descended from me, that my name goes on forever, and that Jesus actually sat and still sits on the throne of David. The throne of David is in heaven, and the realization that Jesus is called the Son of David tremendously excites and invigorates me.

An appropriate description and comparison to how I feel is how beautiful a bride feels on her wedding day in her wedding dress as she walks up to her husband or how she feels in the official photos, including the one as she signs the marriage license. As she nervously walks up to her husband and says her vows, as she cuts the cake, as she appears in the official photographs, she's overcome with pride and love for her husband and unmatched excitement. Many women say that their wedding day was the best memory of their life. I feel like that bride, extra-special and the center of attention. I feel that I was greatly honored by God. I had the favor of God on my life. I excelled at everything that I did. So many things that I did had God's favor on them, and his wisdom carried me.

As I already said, Solomon wanted wisdom because I possessed great wisdom myself. You'll find a lot of wisdom in my Psalms. You'll find that I was amazingly intimate with God.

Psalm 111:10 says that the fear of God is the beginning of wisdom, and I certainly had a reverential fear of God and respect for him. I exemplified what it is to be a servant and to be a king who ruled with God's glory, power, and ability. And heaven knows my past; heaven knows the role I played in the events of mankind. Heaven is very aware of what a great patriarch I was in the annals of history in the Bible. The people of heaven are very much aware of why Jesus descended from me and why he was called the Son of David.

I truly modelled perfection and the spirit of excellence. I hope that, as you read this book or listen to it on Audible, you can capture a portion of my wisdom. I pray that you can capture my voice and discern my personality and that I am a wise, loving, and compassionate person. I certainly desire for you to come into a relationship with God that is similar to mine, that you can draw near to God and to Jesus. Jesus might not ever be called your son, but you can worship and draw close to him and reach a point in life where he is as proud of you as he was of me.

Question 16: What is your favorite thing about heaven, and what are your favorite things to do there?

In answer to your question, my favorite thing about heaven and my favorite thing to do there are the same thing. I imagine you could guess my answer. What do you think, dear reader, that I would enjoy the most in heaven? What is heaven renowned for? What happens in heaven that most Christians know about?

The answer to that is worship. Nothing pleases me more than to worship God and to worship Jesus. I find tremendous joy in being in the presence of God and lying down prostrate before him and worshipping him. Sometimes I just cry! Sometimes the presence of God comes on me so strongly that I weep. Sometimes I stand up and worship.

Often, I'll even be used to lead worship in heaven. In heaven, your voice is louder than all the other voices when you lead worship, so you don't need a microphone. Many times, I've been asked to lead worship in heaven and not be a worshipper in the congregation. I've found over the years that I have an ability to let myself go and worship God in such a way that I carry everyone into an ecstatic, amazing experience. Other people can also lead worship in heaven. I'm not the only person who leads worship, but I really enjoy it. I enjoy being one of the worshippers in the congregation just as much as leading. I love to worship. My whole life in heaven revolves around that.

Of course, I do other things: eat, meet people, associate with them, talk to them, answer their questions, come alongside them, and encourage them. I like to help people progress in their relationship with God and with Jesus. I enjoy speaking to God, conversing with him, sitting by him, and discussing various topics. I enjoy participating in the councils of heaven where we decide about different events on earth and make decisions. I enjoy showing people the glory of God.

I enjoy teaching classes on worship. I enjoy instructing people how to enter in and how to worship better. I enjoy training musicians, counseling, and teaching musicians how to write worship songs. I like to find people who are new to writing music and teach them how to construct lyrics and melodies and how to write and play music. I'm proud to say that some of my students have gone on to write "The Best Worship Song" in heaven for the week and be celebrated.

I've taken people with little or no ability when they reached heaven and trained them to write beautiful music. Of course, the person's ability to write a quality worship song comes down to their heart and is not so much about their musical ability or their talent. The more refined their relationship is with Jesus and with the Father, the more devoted and the more in love they are with Jesus and the Father, the purer their music is. You can have people who are exceptionally skilled in music, who are artistically talented, and who have a great voice with perfect pitch, and they don't win "The Best Worship Song" in heaven. The competition is very challenging as everyone who is a musician plays against each other. Talent doesn't win it; it's won by the heart, the worshipper's heart that writes beautiful music and songs that touch the very heart of God and the worshippers in heaven.

For example, Michael Jackson had the heart; he truly loved Jesus. It didn't take him many years in heaven to be able to write a song that was voted the best in heaven for the week because he had this pure, unadulterated, beautiful heart and was able to transpose his talent into focusing on writing a worship song for God that blessed the heart of God and the people of heaven.

I'm pleased to say that I've won "The Best Song in Heaven" quite a few times. This contest is not a week in heaven time but in earth's time. In heaven, I have a new song that's being prepared for competition. Michael Jackson has to compete against me, and I've been writing worship songs for thousands of years. It's not an easy feat to come to heaven and to beat me or to beat one or the other worshippers there. As talented and as popular as Michael was on earth, his heart is certainly to write a song of excellence in heaven. I enjoy worship and teaching worship in heaven. I enjoy instructing people, mixing with them, loving them, and growing close to God with the community there. These are some of the things that I enjoy. I hope, Mary, that I answered your question sufficiently.

Question 17: Can you describe how you felt when you were anointed king of Israel at such a young age?

When I was anointed king of Israel, I was like a child who was given the keys to a palace. If you had a palace with two hundred staff and you were responsible to lead the whole of Israel, it would be a big deal. You could compare this today to if you were made queen and then given a palace with all the luxury cars and the staff. It would be overwhelming to a young boy. Likewise, it was overwhelming for me. I was pleased to meet Samuel but quite intimidated in one sense to be called before my family when he anointed me as king. Certainly, I understood the significance of what was happening. I understood what I was being called to do. But I felt somewhat unworthy and totally unprepared and inexperienced. To use a cliché, I felt like I was thrown into the deep end of a pool over my head.

From the time I was anointed to many years later, I struggled. It was exciting in one way but so overwhelming. How could you describe it? It's as if you were chosen to represent your country in a sport in the Olympics with the related pressures. I imagine your modern-day Olympians feel that pressure and the weight of responsibility to represent a country in such an important contest when the stakes are so high. I don't want to minimize how I felt. I don't want to devalue or disappoint you in any way, Mary, by saying that I wasn't jubilant or overcome because I was elated at such an honor.

I communicated with God and had a vital relationship with him. When the anointing oil flowed over me, I felt his presence. I felt fully anointed and more in touch with God than many people would feel.

It was an exciting time, but I had to grow into it. I have to say that I had to go through the years in Saul's house and Saul's palace, and I had to go through the years of being pursued by Saul. This season matured me and fashioned me into a man who could handle responsibility, a man who could handle power and authority. I feel that, even though it was hard, taxing, and so stressful for me to go through all those years of being pursued, it was necessary for my growth and character. Although I had a great relationship with the Lord and was very intimate with God, I was unprepared, immature, and not tested.

When you become a Christian, you become a son of God, an heir and adopted into God's family. But your identity is tested as you go through trials, hardships, and struggles. When you fully acknowledge that you're a son with all the rights of a son, and you go through trials and difficulties in life, this tests your relationship as a son. You develop maturity, confidence, and assurance through these tests that you are truly a son. And when you step into that identity and fully relate to it, then you can make decisions that can thwart the enemy and overcome difficulties. You can do miraculous works from that place, from the confidence in your identity. Many Christians never walk in the identity of a son or in the full potential of their strength and ability.

The same was true of me as a young child when I was anointed king of Israel. The throne was rightfully mine as a prophet had anointed me. But I first needed to fully develop and go through all the trials. Once King Saul finally died, I could walk in and become the king that God had destined me to become because of my maturity and strength of character.

Question 18: Why do you think King Saul eventually agreed to let you fight Goliath?

The best answer to this is that he had no choice. The soldiers of Israel were totally intimidated by Goliath. Matthew heard from a teacher recently that Goliath might have been as high as twelve feet tall, and you imagine that he weighed a proportionate amount at the same time. So he was a very imposing figure. I'm not even six feet tall, so he was double my height. How could you even raise a sword to his upper chest when you're so small in comparison? There's little wonder why Saul wanted me to wear his armor because I was in an impossible situation.

Saul understood my anointing and sensed the Spirit of God on me. You remember, I used to play the harp for Saul, and the presence of God came upon him. He knew that God was with me. When you have the favor of God in your life, people recognize that favor. They might not be able to identify it or put their finger on what it is, but they know that there's something special about you. They certainly recognize the authority and the power that you walk in.

Saul wasn't dumb. He didn't lack understanding or wisdom, and he knew that I carried something special. He had spoken to me and knew that I fought lions and bears, and I singlehandedly protected the sheep from those animals. He knew that I had no fear. The very fact that I was asking to fight Goliath showed that I lacked the fear that his soldiers had. He knew that I was inexperienced in battle. He knew that I was merely a child. He knew that I was a long shot. I have to say that he didn't have absolute confidence that I would succeed in the mission. But no one else in his army volunteered to fight Goliath. No one had the confidence, and he saw a glimmer of hope in me. He saw what God saw in me. He was able to identify something special in me.

In one way, God spoke to him. He was anointed, so God could speak to him, and God gave him the assurance and the go-ahead to move forward with this plan. Of course, God in his foreknowledge knew that I would be the future king. I was anointed as king by God. God reassured Saul that I was the best man—or child—for the job. It was a very interesting turn of events. I'm not fully sure that anything would be different today if your country faced an army with giants during war. Goliath was probably the most ferocious of the giants. But the Philistines certainly had many giants, not just Goliath. So they were an imposing and scary army to face.

In today's warfare, you fight with guns, explosives, bombs, and all sorts of artillery. In those days, we fought with swords and hand-to-hand combat. If a modern army were faced with a similar situation (hand-to-hand combat with a giant on the other side), the same scene would play out today. Faced with an army of giants, an army today would go through fear and trepidation like the nation of Israel did (unless they are Navy SEALs). Taking a historical story and putting it into today's reality gives you a new perspective. You say, "Well, how would we cope if we were facing a twelve-foot giant? How would we deal with the situation? Would we cope with the situation any differently than how I dealt with it when I lived?"

Sometimes people can look at a story like that and say that it was just a story or that I was remarkable. They think that I was successful because I was filled with God's heart, strength, and courage, which made me noble and able to do what I did. But facing Goliath was scary; I had to have the confidence of God on my side to face him down. He was imposing. I don't want you to in any way diminish the fact or misunderstand that only God's confidence and the assurance that God was my Savior and deliverer gave me the courage and the ability to face Goliath.

Question 19: Can you describe your greatest accomplishment as the king of Israel?

You might have noticed when reading the Bible that it mentions the kings of Israel, including the name of the king, when he reigned, and if he served the Lord well or if he was evil in the sight of the Lord. My greatest accomplishment was leading Israel to obey and live under the law of God. I did not allow any foreign temples or worship of foreign gods during my reign. The people of God obeyed the law of God and were happy. We had many times of war in my kingdom along with times of peace and times of distress, but we served God, and the people of God were happy and treated well. They weren't taxed harshly, and a great burden was not put on them.

Scripture says that Solomon put a great burden on the people of God, heavily taxing them, and they were unhappy. (See 1 Kings 12:4.) But the people of God, the children of Israel, were happy under my reign and were happy with me. My greatest accomplishment was that I served God and led his people so that God's heart was very happy.

I want to repeat the phrase; I was a man after God's own heart. I honestly sought to please God in every dimension, in every possible way. My heart was set to please God, and everything that I did in my kingdom, everything that the nation of Israel did under my reign, was well pleasing to God. Our worship, our obedience to God, came up to his nostrils as sweet incense. He was tremendously satisfied with our sacrifices, with our ordinances, with what we did, and the way that we carried on with our lives. God was very pleased with us, and 2 Samuel 22:25 recorded that I pleased the heart of God as a king. God even forgave kings that came after me and showed them grace when they didn't perform well because of his love for me and because of his memory of me. I made God very happy, which made me feel pleased, contented, and encouraged in my own spirit.

Dear reader, that's all God asks of you—to do your very best. He understands that living without sinning is a hard thing to do although it's not impossible. You can live a life that's nearly free from sin. You know, 2 Corinthians 5:17 teaches that you are a new creation, and old things have passed away. The Bible teaches that you can live a life of freedom from sin. (See 1 John 3:6.) But as God is your God and Jesus is your Savior, God wants you to do the very best that you can do. He wants you to live in a state of grace. He wants you to live from a place of rest. He wants you to not strive so hard each day to do your very best and to perform for him, but he wants you to understand that you're a son. He wants you to understand that you're a brother or sister of Jesus and that you've been adopted into his family. He wants you to know that you're loved, and he loves you with a love that actually hurts his heart. He is so in love with you that he weeps.

He wants you to know that you're special to him. Just like the Israelites were God's people, you, as a Christian, are part of the family of God. You are his people, and he wants to lead you. As your God, he wants Jesus to be the center of your life. He wants you to come under the reign and the lordship of Jesus. He wants you to commit your ways to him and live your life so that it is well pleasing to him. He wants you to fully relax and rest in his love and be confident that he loves you, assured that he has your very best interests at heart.

My greatest accomplishment was to give the people of Israel a sense of security, a sense of protection, and a sense of contentment that they were serving God and that they were well pleasing to him. God could use my songs and my worship to encourage the people of God, the Israelites. With the knowledge that God was well pleased and happy, I tremendously enjoyed leading worship, being a king, and leading the people of Israel to serve God with all their heart, dedicated to him.

Question 20: Can you describe the darkest hour of your life? What advice can you give people today on how to overcome heartaches, trials, and attacks from our enemies? What advice do you have for someone who suffers from depression?

One of my darkest hours was when the people of God at Ziklag turned on me and wanted to stone me. That was a very hard time for me. I also struggled when Saul was pursuing me for all those years. So many times, I was overcome with thoughts of not wanting to continue, thoughts of giving in, thoughts of giving up, and turning myself in to Saul so that he could kill me. It was difficult to go on and to persevere. Can you imagine being anointed as king, to rightfully be the king and yet still be denied that job?

A couple of times, I was given the opportunity to kill Saul, but I didn't kill him. Both times, I told him that I was given the opportunity to kill him, but I didn't take advantage of it. Once, I took his drink and his sword, and I shouted, "I took these things, and I could've killed you. I came right beside you, and I didn't kill you. Now back off and leave me alone and stop pursuing me!" (See 1 Samuel 26:12.) Saul wouldn't listen to me, and he wouldn't listen to the Lord. He persisted in pursuing me.

What advice can I give people today to overcome trials and attacks of our enemies? You live in a difficult world. Take comfort in God.

From time to time, Matthew will receive harsh reviews on his books. From time to time, people will call him out in a thread on Facebook and argue with him, speaking negatively. Matthew simply blocks people that come against him so that they can't speak any further poison to him. You know, the Lord says to forgive people and turn the other cheek, but when given the opportunity to remove someone from your life who's harassing you or causing you trouble, the best option is sometimes to block them.

Sometimes it's best to forgive people from a distance and to cut them out of your life so that you don't have to keep dealing with them.

If you are struggling with a person at work and you can't get rid of them by leaving your work or moving away, you can deal with the situation by praying for the person. As you pray for the person and seek an understanding of the person's heart and where the person is coming from, you can ask the Lord to give you insight into how he feels about the person, what he thinks of the person, and how he loves the person. As you receive insight about where they're coming from and about how God feels about them, you will have a renewed understanding of the person. With that new knowledge from the Lord, you will have further insight into God's perspective and a better idea of how to deal with the person and how to cope with them.

I understand that life has struggles. If you have learned anything from my life, from reading about me, or from reading the Psalms, you'll know that I suffered all of my life with many trials. I had heartaches, troubles, struggles, and enemies all through my life. I persevered, and I wrote the most worship songs that were ever written in history. I wrote so many more psalms than those recorded in the Bible. I wrote so many songs. I made it a habit to run to God, which is what I suggest that you do when you have struggles, trials, difficulties, and hardships. I suggest that you develop a relationship with God and run to him.

As for people with depression, you can take medication. Matthew attended Freedom Encounters, which can be found at the following link: https://www.freedomencounters.com They prayed for him to be delivered from demonic spirits. He used to suffer from regular bouts of depression, but they have mostly left his life. From time to time, he will be depressed for a little while, but he no longer struggles to the same extent that he used to suffer before he went through deliverance. I encourage you to check out Freedom Encounters and go through deliverance. The enemy hates you, and if you suffer from depression, he wants to keep you in bondage. Matthew found success through Freedom Encounters, and you would probably find success through them as well so that the demonic influence in your life can be broken and eradicated once and for all.

So if you suffer, struggle, or have enemies, my best and surest suggestion and what worked for me is to run to the Lord and develop a strong and intimate relationship with Jesus and with God the Father. Through your intimacy, through the depth and strength of your relationship with Jesus and with the Father, you'll be able to cope with nearly everything. With a great relationship with God, all things are possible.

Question 21: If you could live your life over again, what would you change and do differently?

I had no regrets. I feel that the best way to live your life on earth is to keep short accounts with God. That means, in every situation and in every part of your life, to be sure to take things to God and process things with him. Some people might look at my life and look at this question and say, "Surely you wouldn't have slept with Bathsheba; surely you wouldn't have committed adultery and killed her husband. If you relived your life, surely you wouldn't have done those things."

Jesus was descended from Bathsheba. Solomon was one of the greatest men who ever lived. If Solomon hadn't been born, the world would have been different. Before Jesus, Solomon was the wisest man who lived on earth. Would you like it if your history books did not include the life of Solomon? Would you like it if your Bible did not include Proverbs?

You must live a life where you confess sin to God, walking out your life with understanding and grace. I wouldn't change anything in my life. The short answer to that question is that I am happy with the life that I lived. Killing a man (Uriah) and committing adultery with his wife (Bathsheba) seems to be unforgivable from the perspective of man. Yet even so, God chose to make my throne an everlasting throne. Even so, God chose to call Jesus a Son of David. You have to consider why that is so.

Why is someone who committed adultery and murder celebrated as one of the best people that ever lived? It really comes down to looking at how man looks at each other. Man never seems to forget sin; man looks at sin and can't forgive or forget it. When you look at the life of Peter, how he sank in the water and how he denied Jesus three times, Peter is remembered for saying that he'll never desert Jesus but then going on to deny him three times.

Many sermons on Peter are the stories of his denial of Jesus three times. Man can't seem to forget errors or shortfalls in a person's life. Very rarely do people preach that Peter's shadow healed the multitudes when people got underneath his shadow. Not many people in the world walk in so much anointing that, wherever they go, wherever their shadow falls on people, people are healed. I don't know of anyone today who walks in that level of anointing.

I wouldn't change a thing in my life. It takes another sort of person, another level of maturity, to face and deal with your struggles and shortfalls in such a way that you have a renewed look at them with the perspective of the redeeming grace of Jesus.

You should live life so that you can say, "I have no regrets." Can you actually say that? Reader, can you look at your life and honestly say that you have no regrets? Or are there things that you'd rather not have done, things that you wish were not on your conscience? Why are they on your conscience? Why do you feel badly about them? Hasn't Jesus forgiven them?

You know, Psalm 103:12 says that he removes our sins as far as the east is from the west. Scripture says in Micah 7:19 that God throws our sins into the sea of forgetfulness and remembers them no more. If God forgives our sins and forgets about them, why can't you forgive yourself? Is it that strange to say, "I was happy with my life? I wouldn't do anything differently if I relived my life." Does that shock you to hear? Are you amazed that I can say that even though I did these horrible things?

Jesus said, "You have heard that it was said to those of old, 'You shall not murder, and whoever murders will be in danger of the judgment.' But I say to you that whoever is angry with his brother without a cause shall be in danger of the judgment. And whoever says to his brother, 'Raca!' shall be in danger of the council. But whoever says, 'You fool!' shall be in danger of hell fire" (Matthew 5:21–22).

Is that true? Are you angry with certain people? Do you hate certain people? Are you as guilty of murder as I was? Jesus said, "You have heard that it was said to those of old, 'You shall not commit adultery.' But I say to you that whoever looks at a woman to lust for her has already committed adultery with her in his heart." (Matthew 5:27–28). Are you as guilty of adultery in your heart?

We must come to an understanding that, yes, we do serve a just God, but we also serve a redeeming God. We also serve a God who makes all things new, a God who restores, forgives, and heals the brokenhearted. We serve a God that transforms and changes the lives of those who follow him, those who worship him, and those who pursue him. I encourage you to ponder my words and marvel that I wouldn't change a thing.

Question 22: What was the biggest impact playing music and singing had in your life?

I was able to worship in Jerusalem, lead the Israelites in worship, and sing with the worship team. I truly enjoyed that, but the biggest impact that playing music and singing had in my life was privately singing and worshipping even apart from my wives. You know, I enjoyed singing to Bathsheba, and she loved it. At times, she wept when I worshipped.

Most of all, I enjoyed privately singing to God, just me and him. I loved playing music and singing, worshipping God all by myself. In heaven, I like worshipping and leading worship in the throne room and leading people in worship. But more than that, I enjoy the worship when I'm in a congregation, just me and God. People might be around, but I disappear into being alone with God. From time to time, I'll walk by myself in heaven beside a stream or beside the Crystal Sea, and I'll sing worship to God alone. I enjoy being alone and worshipping God.

I've always enjoyed worshipping God and Jesus and letting them know that I love them. From time to time as I'm worshipping, walking by streams, by the Crystal Sea, or alone in nature in heaven, God will speak to me. We'll have a conversation. I'll worship him, and we'll have another conversation. And then I'll worship him once again. It's such a special time. Dad especially loves me and delights in me. My own father is in heaven along with my brothers. When I mention *Dad*, Matthew thought of my natural dad. So all my family's in heaven.

If you're not a worshipper and if you only worship at church on Sundays or when you go to church, you might not understand my heart like someone would understand who is a worship leader or a musician. Someone who's a real worshipper, whose whole life is devoted to worship, will understand how I enjoy being alone and worshipping God. It means so much to me.

Matthew read about a tabernacle made in heaven especially for me. I do have my own tabernacle in heaven where I worship. Not many people know that about me, but Matthew especially trusts the person who wrote that. I spend time alone in the tabernacle and worship God because God doesn't need a sacrifice anymore, but he enjoys a sacrifice of praise. He truly enjoys people worshipping him and spending time prostrate before him, singing their hearts out to him. He loves it when I spend time lifting up his name in heaven. I'm happy to announce that I bring God joy.

So many things are happening on earth that distress and upset God. So much pain is in God's heart and in his life when he looks at earth and sees the suffering there and hears the cries of people. I wish I could explain to you how much pain God goes through when people suffer.

Matthew has three books to date: <u>Conversations with God: Book 1</u>, <u>Conversations with God: Book 2</u>, and <u>Conversations with God: Book 3</u>. In them, God shares some of his heart, and perhaps you might want to read them. It might help you to know that, in the midst of his pain and suffering, God experiences joy. I'm so pleased that I bring God joy in heaven and that I brought him joy when I lived on earth. I filled his heart with happiness. I'm very pleased that I still make him happy.

My life on earth was a continual expression of worship. Every part of my life involved laying down my life and being separated to God. I didn't just worship from time to time, but I lived a lifestyle of worship. I encourage you to live the same way.

Question 23: What advice can you give Christians who are trying to live a holy life for God today?

If you don't know why you're here or what your purpose is, you can't enjoy your life like you should. If you have no understanding of why you were created and what you were created to do, you can't truly lead a wonderful life. Life can be difficult and trying for you if you don't know your purpose and if you're not living and walking in it. It can be a hard labor, challenging to process.

So many people focus on living a holy and a righteous life. If they know why they're here and they know their purpose, they will find that it's a lot easier to live a righteous life and live a life that pleases God. He is pleased when you're doing what you were created to do. I can't seem to emphasize that enough! So you need to find out why you're here.

You can take a spiritual gifts test or take the [MYERS-BRIGGS TYPE INDICATOR®](#) personality assessment, which will tell you about your personality type and will tell you what some of your gifts are. You can find out more in Matthew's book, *Finding Your Purpose in Christ*. I suggest that you read that book to learn how to understand your purpose.

Besides knowing your purpose in Christ, you can live a holy and righteous life today by developing an intimate relationship with Jesus. Intimacy with Jesus will help you achieve many things.

Jesus and God both love you for who you are. If you're struggling with a certain sin and you have trouble overcoming it, focusing on that sin all the time actually makes matters worse. When you come to a strong understanding that Jesus loves you despite the sin and forgives you regardless of what you're going through, you can then conquer that sin. You can overcome sin and walk in holiness and righteousness through the empowering grace of God. So I encourage you to pay attention to what I have to say.

The pilot keys in a plane's destination and then switches on the autopilot. The plane then flies itself to the destination. When you have an intimate relationship with Jesus and you know why you're here, your life is switched to autopilot and goes in the right direction. Little effort is required on your part. The same is true for you when it comes to living a life of holiness. When you know why you're here and when you do what you are called to do, you won't need to try to be holy. When you have an intimate relationship with Jesus, you won't be burned out, and holiness will come naturally. When your purpose and your relationship with Jesus are in place, the rest will follow.

The analogy of a pilot, a plane, and autopilot helps explain that you need to put these points together in order to head in the right direction.

Question 24: We've read in the Bible how you killed bears and the giant, Goliath. What advice can you give people today in fighting the giants in their lives?

The most powerful element that you can have in your life is faith. God responds to faith. If you go to a healing meeting and you meet a successful healer, you might not be healed if you have doubt in your heart. It's very sad, but that happens. We sometimes wish that God didn't need our faith. We wish that the healer's faith was enough for us, which sometimes does happen.

When Peter healed the man at the Gate Beautiful at the entrance to the temple courts, he didn't have faith to be healed. (See Acts 3:2.) He only wanted money, and Peter's faith healed him. The man who was in the Pool of Bethesda, waiting for the angel to stir the water, didn't have faith either. But Jesus healed him too. (See John 5:1–15.) Faith is such an important element. God responds to faith. So many times when you're faced with a challenge or a trial, you need faith to overcome. The difference between a normal trial and a giant is that a giant seems like it's impossible to overcome.

So many promises are found in different passages in the Bible. One promise in the Bible that Matthew knows well is in Psalm 1. Psalm 1:3 says this, "He shall be like a tree planted by the rivers of water, that brings forth its fruit in its season, whose leaf also shall not wither; and whatever he does shall prosper."

The Bible makes this promise to us. This person is "like a tree planted by the rivers of water" so that his or her whole life is fed by the water of the Holy Spirit. He or she brings forth "fruit in his season," abundant fruit. He's full of answers for everyone who needs answers. "His leaf shall not wither." Despite circumstances, despite drought, despite times when there's a lack of water, a lack of sustenance, the "leaf shall not wither" and will never cease from being green. "And whatever he does shall prosper." Whatever that person turns their hands to will prosper and see success. That's an example of a promise in the Bible.

All of the promises in the Bible are true. The start of Psalm 1 is the condition because so many of the promises of God have conditions. Psalm 1:1–2 reads as follows: "Blessed is the man who walks not in the counsel of the ungodly, nor stands in the path of sinners, nor sits in the seat of the scornful; But his delight is in the law of the Lord, and in His law he meditates day and night."

This person is blessed who doesn't mix with people who are sinful or ungodly or who stand in the path of sinners, who don't congregate with them or stand in their way. His life isn't a bad example; it is a life that leads people to Christ.

"Nor sits in the seat of the scornful." This person doesn't sit with people who are mockers, those who mock God and mock leadership. This person doesn't hang around ungodly people or Christians who are full of pride and who think they are better than their pastors and everyone else, who think that they are amazing and that everyone else is a jerk.

"But his delight is in the law of the Lord." His delight is in the Word of God and in his law, and he meditates on the Word of God day and night. He continually concentrates on the promises of God. If this person does all of that, then he will be like verse 3 that says, "He shall be like a tree planted by the rivers of water, that brings forth its fruit in its season, whose leaf also shall not wither; and whatever he does shall prosper."

So my message to you is that, in order to fulfill that promise, you have to do the work. You can't be hanging around sinners and ungodly people or Christians who are not achieving anything, including gossipers, complainers, or mockers. You can't hang around those people and expect to be blessed with the promise. If people like that are a part of your life, you are better off with no friends as opposed to having friends like that.

Blessing comes with a cost. Every difficult situation and every obstacle can be overcome with faith in a specific promise that speaks to that difficulty. So many promises in the Bible refer to impossible situations, and you need to see the condition of the promise and fulfill it.

"Trust in the Lord with all your heart, and lean not on your own understanding; in all your ways acknowledge Him, and He shall direct your paths" (Proverbs 3:5–6). This verse refers to your heart, which is your spirit. Trust in God with your intuition, with what your heart is saying, and don't trust what your mind is saying or lean "on your own understanding." If you divorce your mind and trust your spirit that you can overcome, you will overcome. But if you let your mind dominate, your mind might lie to you that you are facing a giant that can't be overcome. You won't overcome if you listen to those thoughts. But if you listen to your spirit and engage in the promise, the Lord will perfect your ways and make your paths straight.

God responds to your faith, and if you have faith that you can overcome a giant, you can speak to the mountain and overcome it. Jesus said, "Speak to the mountain, and it will move." (See Mark 11:23.) You can actually name the mountain—a difficult employer at work, an abusive or violent spouse, bills that need to be paid—

and speak to it and tell the mountain to change or disappear. If you do that with faith, with assurance that you believe with all of your heart, you can see drastic results. I know that it's hard. Life is difficult, and yet you can overcome problems. My faith in God alone allowed me to overcome Goliath. Thank you, Mary, for all your questions. You certainly blessed the readers and allowed me to share more of my life.

Rebecca's Questions

Question 25: You had amazing faith in God when you faced Goliath. Why were you so confident?

Hello, Rebecca. I'm very pleased to make your acquaintance. I hope you enjoy this book.

As you were saying, I had amazing faith when I faced Goliath. It's true; I did. We've discussed that Goliath was twelve feet tall, and he was very broad across his chest. He was overpowering and too big for someone like me, who was less than six feet tall, to fight with a sword. It was impossible for me to beat Goliath in sword-to-sword combat. But I was not a stranger to the impossible. It's impossible for a person to fight a lion in a hand-to-hand battle and win. It's impossible for a man to fight a bear in hand-to-hand combat and win. I had those earlier successes. I had operated in the power and in the anointing of God against those dangerous animals and succeeded.

I can't say that my brothers would have succeeded as well as I did with my background as a shepherd. I had tremendous faith in God. When I picked up those five stones, I believed that I could kill Goliath with only one stone. I was confident in my abilities. But more than confident in my abilities, I was confident in my God—that he was an overcoming God. I was confident in his character. Let's face it, that's what people lack. When people don't see miracles, when they don't see God come through for them, it's because they have a wrong understanding of God's character.

If you believe the following:

- God is a God that loves you

- Through the covenant of the blood of Jesus, his blood can heal you of all diseases

- God is a good God with many promises for us and

- God's a God of laws and justice,

then you can have the faith to heal people or to be healed yourself. But when you hold God in any less regard than who he actually is, when you have a misconception of his character, then you might struggle. People sometimes falsely represent the character of God and think that God wants to see individuals and even groups of people suffer.

In the United States, the people raised up and voted in a leader that they believed in during the 2016 election. The people of God turned out to vote for change, according to their faith. Their voting caused the miracle. All the polls and all the news reports in America were saying that Donald Trump wouldn't win. If the people believed the news reports instead of believing in the character of God, they wouldn't have even turned out to vote. They wouldn't have even tried to change the result. But so many Christians prayed and had faith in God that he was going to deliver their nation from the hands of evildoers. The Christians' faith in God and in his character saved America. The people's supernatural faith in God brought them their deliverer, Donald Trump.

The same was true with my relationship with God. I believed that God would deliver the Israelites out of the hands of Goliath. Goliath had proposed that the Israelites send one fighter to represent Israel and if that fighter won against him, then the Philistines would be conquered by the Israelites. He suggested that just one representative from each country would fight each other rather than have everyone in both armies fight and lose many people. Whoever won the battle won for the whole country. Goliath put himself up as the representative for his country. As you know, I was the representative for Israel. Then I won and Israel won. I had faith in God to be my deliverer, fortress, and savior. My faith prevailed and ignited the acceleration of that stone into Goliath's skull. The faith that I had in God propelled that projectile into Goliath's forehead. The strength of my faith—not a stone—killed Goliath. My undeniable faith in God prevailed that day.

I'm saddened to say that many Christians don't have that kind of faith. Many Christians could not confidently stand face to face with a twelve-foot giant and have faith that they would succeed. Even some of your best preachers might not have that faith. As a reader, consider if you would have the faith to face down a twelve-foot giant in hand-to-hand combat. If I gave you a slingshot, would you have the faith to take him down? If your answer is "no," then you need to do some work to increase your faith.

Question 26: When you sinned by killing Bathsheba's husband, did you think that God wasn't watching?

That's a very interesting question, Rebecca. I knew that God saw everything. But I also knew that I was one of God's favorites. In my lack of wisdom, I thought that God would overlook my behavior. I wondered what God could do. I wasn't prepared for Nathan to come and confront me. I was in trouble because Bathsheba was pregnant. I was nervous that her husband would find out and that I'd be called an adulterer. Adultery was still a sin in the land, and I was afraid of being found out by her husband and the people.

I was like a lot of people when they're caught. Many people today in America are being caught for sexual abuse and sexual harassment. They will go to all sorts of lengths to cover and hide their sin. They'll threaten people and their victims; they'll do all sorts of things to keep their sin from being exposed and revealed. The same was true with me; nothing's changed since then. I was in a hard spot. I was aware that God saw what happened. But I was thinking, *Well, God's not going to call me out on this. I'm his king. I can mostly do as I please.* Instead, he called Nathan to confront me and expose my sin.

Then God actually took my first son. Today, he doesn't seem to take a person's son if they commit adultery. I suppose that there are so many abortions now that God can't afford to kill babies. But I was still surprised that Nathan confronted me. I was surprised that I was caught in my sin; I was very embarrassed and ashamed.

Like I've covered, I was quick to repent. I was quick to confess to God that I'd sinned before him. I used to keep short accounts with God. If you're a Christian and you haven't heard the expression "keep short accounts with God," it's the practice of confessing your sins to God as soon as you realize that you've fallen short, as soon as you're aware that you made a sinful decision. When you're convicted by the Holy Spirit, keeping short accounts is actually bringing those things before God as soon as possible to get them off your conscience and to clear up matters between you and God.

People mistakenly think that God turned away his face from Jesus on the cross. But that's not true. The Father watched the crucifixion of his Son. A rabbi used to recite the first line of a psalm or a passage, and all the people knew that the rabbi was going to talk about that passage. They all had memorized that passage, and they recited that passage as the rabbi spoke about it.

When Jesus cried, "Father, Father, why do you deny me?" he was highlighting Psalm 22 for people. This chapter was being fulfilled before their eyes. "For He has not despised nor abhorred the affliction of the afflicted; nor has He hidden His face from Him; but when He cried to Him, He heard" (Psalm 22:24).

Similarly, people think that God turns his head away when we sin. God doesn't turn his head away when we sin, and he doesn't take away his presence from a sinner. But as sinners, we move ourselves away from God and run from him until we've confessed our sins. Keeping short accounts with God is the practice of keeping your relationship sound, healthy, vibrant, and alive.

I recommend that you do not wait days or weeks or even longer to confess your sins but that you keep yourself accountable to God with your heart sensitive and ready to deal with your shortfalls and errors. Keep short accounts with God so that you remain fully blessed. To answer your question, no, I didn't think God would not see the sin, but I definitely didn't think that he would call me on it.

Question 27: How did you write the psalms? What was your favorite psalm?

As a writer, I wrote under my own inspiration and the inspiration of God. Many people compose a Facebook post, and they are inspired by what they've gone through, or they have something on their heart to say. Many times, someone's hurt them, or they've been through bad experiences, and they want to vent. They might want to talk about how they've been hurt or disappointed or share what's happened to them. They write under their own inspiration. Other times, people are inspired by God, which means that the Holy Spirit moves on a person, and they post on Facebook as God inspires them.

The inspiration from a person and the inspiration from the Holy Spirit might even sound the same. A person might say that they don't like church because the church doesn't love people, and people are hypocritical, cruel, and mean. The difference between the two posts is that the one written under the inspiration of the Holy Spirit is a little bit more encouraging but just as hard-hitting. It would convict the reader and bring people to repentance and change people's attitudes. The one inspired by the person can come across as condemning and hurt many people who read it.

I wrote most of the psalms under the inspiration of the Holy Spirit, yet it was also me writing; it was from my heart. I was pouring out my heart on paper. But the Holy Spirit was inspiring my writings. Sometimes, Rebecca, you've probably written words with your own intellect and your own thoughts. And sometimes, you've been inspired by the Holy Spirit and felt his presence and his leading in what you've written. As a writer, Matthew understands what inspires him.

As he has been lying here for close to five hours, recording the answers to these questions, everything has flowed naturally and organically. He's a third party to actually listen to what I'm saying. The thoughts are hardly even coming through his intellect. Most of the answers seem to be just coming from his mouth. He's actually hearing the answers as he speaks them. He's very confident that it's inspired. For a couple of questions, he clenched his teeth and wondered whether it was really inspired when I spoke about having no regrets and the fact that I wouldn't do anything differently.

It was hard for him to accept that I didn't say that I was sorry that I slept with Bathsheba or that I was sorry that I killed her husband. But if I lived my life again, I'd do the same thing. That was hard for him to accept, but he knows most of what I said was truly inspired and truly spoken by me.

He's very confident, and as he sits, he is very happy with the message that I've been giving. He thinks that this is one of the best books he has ever written because it's very comprehensive and inspired and so other worldly. Being inspired takes the book to another level.

Most musicians are inspired when they write music. Many musicians might think that they're going to write a song one day, but they can't get into the flow. In Christian terms, they don't sense the anointing, but even secular writers have to be inspired. They can't just sit down and write a song. If they do write a song without inspiration, it falls flat and doesn't sound right. They don't even continue with the song. They have to have a supernatural experience so that the song comes from a spiritual place in their spirits. The song has to flow from their spirit and must be heartfelt and intuitive. If their intuition isn't working, if they can't get into what they call "the flow of the rhythm," then they can't write good songs.

This is true of secular and Christian artists, and it was true of me. I used to sit down with my diary, and I'd feel inspired and write. Sometimes you can still be inspired when you're depressed. Matthew can write creative poems and other excellent material when he's depressed. So you don't have to be happy-happy, joy-joy, or in the greatest of moods to be inspired. A chronically depressed person can write some very inspired material, and when people read it, they can be cut to the heart and even feel those emotions themselves.

You can also write uplifting and beautiful songs when you're inspired and in good spirits. You can write some sad and depressing lyrics when you're depressed. On the other hand, you can actually be in a good mood but channel a dark mood and write some inspired, depressed lyrics when you're happy. Similarly, you can be depressed and reach a place in yourself where you write some encouraging and uplifting lyrics when you're still depressed. It's definitely an artistic question for those who are writers or who are creative.

It's amazing that the world has made Psalm 23, which is my favorite as I mentioned earlier, their most popular psalm too.

Question 28: You played the harp for Saul. What effect did this have on him?

Saul was troubled by demonic spirits. The Spirit of God had departed from him. I want you to consider how worship music affects you when you play it. Matthew will play worship music on his computer through iTunes. The music puts him in another mood and takes him to another place. Peace and joy settle on his heart. When you go to a church, you don't have to be standing up and worshiping to be affected by the music. Worship can deeply touch you and minister to your heart, filling you with joy and peace.

Yesterday, Matthew watched *The Greatest Showman*, a movie with Hugh Jackman. Hugh sang in the show, a musical, a number of times. When Hugh sang, it took Matthew to another surreal place, and he found himself crying. The experience was so touching. The beauty of the songs was amazing. The same is true when you sit in church during worship, and you're touched and taken to another place. You're taken to another place when you sit at your computer and play iTunes. When you watch a ballet or listen to an opera and you're overcome with emotion, the music touches you deeply.

This all happened to Saul. The anointing on my harp, on my music, on my lyrics, and on my songs deeply touched him. The angels of God came with the presence of God. As I was saying, the anointing of God actually shut down the demons in Saul when I played. He could readily recognize that, without me, he was hopeless. Without me, he was tormented. But the problem was that, once he was not tormented, he forgot about the music. He then used to get his spear and try to pin me to the wall. I had to always be vigilant when I was worshiping and run when his spear was coming.

It's true that worship will take you to another place. It doesn't even have to be anointed but only inspired. An opera, a choir, Michael Jackson, Prince, your favorite artist, or your favorite song can take you to another place. You can be in a sad mood and listen to a song that made you happy when you were sixteen. The song will transport you back to that time, the place of happiness and joy where you didn't have any struggles in life. Music has that ability to transform, to invigorate, to bless, and to encourage a person. I was used as an instrument of the Lord to serve Saul.

It's scary to be anointed by God and then to lose your anointing. It's scary to have the Holy Spirit disappear from your life. You'll notice that in Psalm 51, I said, "Take not your Holy Spirit from me." I definitely didn't want that to happen to me like it happened to Saul. As I have shared, I dearly loved Saul, and I had this pure heart that loved everybody. I was saddened by his torture, saddened by his harassment by demons, and I was only too pleased and honored to come and play the harp for him and soothe some of his pain.

Question 29: What was it like to wait all those years, knowing that you were anointed to be king of Israel but not being able to fulfill your destiny?

I can say that it was a very trying time. It would have been easier to wait to be king of Israel and not to be sitting on the throne if I wasn't being pursued. The hardest thing about those years was hiding in caves, running from Saul's army. My life was threatened, and I was scared and troubled on the run, having to escape sightings. Saul had spies and people looking all around for me and my men. Ordinary citizens would give us up and report us. Saul was always after us, and it was very hard to stay joyful. But my life parallels many other people's lives.

Matthew had a prophecy when he was fourteen that he would one day travel in a plane, and his church would go to the airport and see him off on a preaching trip. That hasn't happened yet.

Matthew is now fifty-one. It's been thirty-seven years, and he has been waiting all this time. He's had many prophecies about traveling the world, teaching, and being a prophet to the nations, and yet, so far, only his books have traveled the world. Matthew hasn't physically traveled the world yet. To all those people who have been prophesied over that they will do great and mighty things, be encouraged. Many of you have waited five, ten, and twenty years, and the prophecies haven't been fulfilled yet.

You can consider my life and all the years that I was waiting from the time I was anointed until I became king. The waiting can be an example to you, speaking into your life. If God spoke to you, telling you that something would happen, it'll happen. If God spoke to you and prophesied it to you, confirming the word through other prophetic voices, he will clearly do what he has said. But it takes time for those things to come to pass.

I learned patience. Patience is interesting. You can't receive the gift of patience. Someone can't just pray for you to be filled with patience. Patience has to be exercised and developed, and I certainly developed and learned it over the years. I was in constant communion with God, talking to him. I was anointed. I had open communication with God so that he could reassure me about the future. If I was impatient and not trusting God as I waited to be king, if my faith was in myself and not in God, I would have killed Saul when I had two opportunities to do so.

Many men on earth supplant their leadership. Many men take steps to be promoted themselves. Many people call themselves prophets and apostles, but they aren't. Many people have ministries but work in their own strength. If I didn't have the patience in God, if I didn't trust in him, then I would have killed Saul and taken matters into my own hands. The people would have forgiven me for killing Saul, and I would have been appointed as king. But the mere fact that I didn't kill Saul when I was given the opportunity meant that I trusted in God. I had absolute faith in him to come through for me and to do what he said. Saul and Jonathan eventually died in a battle that they were not to enter into. As soon as they died, I was appointed king of Israel.

I reigned in Judah for seven years and in Jerusalem over all Israel and Judah for thirty-three years—a total of forty years. (See 2 Samuel 5:5.) The number forty is a special number. I was pleased to be a righteous king that reigned that long. The few years that I waited to be king were nothing compared to the forty years of reigning. A lot of years passed in between when I was anointed king as a boy and when my reign as king ended.

I hope that I answered your questions sufficiently, Rebecca. Thank you so much for asking them so that people could get to know me better.

Matthew's Question

Question 30: David, what are your final words?

I'd like to say, Matthew, that I thoroughly enjoyed myself today. I enjoyed speaking to you and through you. It's been a real privilege to come down and share my thoughts with people. I encourage you, if you're a Christian, to go through the Bible and read about my life and the experiences that I had. Come back to this book and read it one more time. Soak in the wisdom that I shared, and understand that you need to live a life where you keep short accounts with God. I encourage you to pray to Jesus every day and confess your sins. I encourage you to learn how to worship Jesus.

I encourage you to draw close to Jesus by reading *7 Keys to Intimacy with Jesus*, Matthew's book. Develop a relationship with him. You can learn more about Jesus in *Finding Intimacy with Jesus Made Simple* or *Jesus Speaking Today*, two other books written by Matthew. I encourage you to get to know God through *Conversations with God: Book 1*, *Conversations with God: Book 2*, and *Conversations with God: Book 3*. I encourage you to learn how to speak to God and to Jesus, which you can do if you read *How to Hear God's Voice*, written by Matthew.

It was a tremendous pleasure to speak to you today. It filled me with joy. It's been an exercise of love for Matthew. It's taken five hours for him to record all of these. Each of the questions was answered one after the other in nine minutes or less of recording time. Every time he finished one, he wrote down the number, saved it, started a new file, and began to record again. When he received the questions from Nicola, Mary, and Rebecca, he was overwhelmed at the number of questions and at how long it would take him to record the book.

I came down to him and spoke to him as he walked to the gas station to get some soda. I reassured him that he'd do fine and that everything would go smoothly. I told him that I was happy with him. I was able to watch him interact with the sales clerk, and I told him that it was great to see him from heaven but that I was happy to be on earth and see him interact with people. I'm so encouraged that you've read this book. If you're listening to this book on Audible, I'm thrilled that you took the time to listen.

I'm just a simple person. I was greatly favored and honored by God because Jesus sits on my throne and was called the Son of David. This is overwhelming to me. It's a real blessing to be called a man after God's own heart and is very encouraging and humbling. I encourage you all to become men and women after God's own heart. I encourage you to pursue God with everything that's within you. I encourage you to try and develop the heart of God and have the heart of God toward other people.

I hope that my story has inspired you to pursue Jesus with all your heart. I hope that the answers to these questions have led you to a more complete understanding of my life. I hope you developed an ability to see the writing between the lines and see some comprehensive answers to some of the things that I faced in my life in some of the situations I encountered. I hope that you've come to understand me more completely as a person and now understand that I was a real human being. I struggled with many issues and went through trials and temptations.

When it comes to struggling, you only have to look at the book of Psalms and read how often I had trouble and how often I was in difficult situations. Everybody has struggles, trials, issues, and problems that harass them and beat them down.

The enemy's objective in your life is to destroy you, to cut you down, and to make you ineffective so that you give up and give in. Many times, I could've given up and given in through all the years that Saul chased me. I was heartbroken and in distress many times. I struggled. Even when I was king, I had so many enemies, and many people came against me. We covered that one of my sons slept with his sister, and Absalom killed him. Then Absalom tried to take my throne from me. Imagine having your own son trying to displace you and hunt you down. It was embarrassing and scary.

Am I happy with who I was? I was very happy about who I was. Am I happy in heaven? I'm overjoyed here. I encourage you all to live a life worthy of your calling. I encourage you all to find the purpose for your life. I hope that I've inspired you to make a goal of pursuing Jesus and becoming intimate with him. I look forward to seeing you all in heaven. If you are worship leaders and musicians, I look forward to teaching you and instructing you in worship and encouraging you to write songs that are worthy of heaven to sing.

I'd love to hear from you

One of the ways that you can bless me as a writer is by writing an honest and candid review of my book on Amazon. I always read the reviews of my books, and I would love to hear what you have to say about this one.

Before I buy a book, I read the reviews first. You can make an informed decision about a book when you have read enough honest reviews from readers. One way to help me sell this book and to give me positive feedback is by writing a review for me. It doesn't cost you a thing but helps me and the future readers of this book enormously.

To read my blog, request a life-coaching session, request your own personal prophecy, request a visit to heaven, or to receive a personal message from your angel, you can also visit my website at http://personal-prophecy-today.com All of the funds raised through my ministry website will go toward the books that I write and self-publish.

You can also request a trip to heaven with Robin Gann. You can find her contact information on my website.

To write to me about this book or to share any other thoughts, please feel free to contact me at my personal email address at survivors.sanctuary@gmail.com

You can also friend request me on Facebook at Matthew Robert Payne. Please send me a message if we have no friends in common as a lot of scammers now send me friend requests.

You can also do me a huge favor and share this book on Facebook as a recommended book to read. This will help me and other readers.

How to Sponsor a Book Project

If you have been blessed by this book, perhaps you might consider sponsoring a book for me. It normally costs me between $1,500 and $2,000 or more to produce each book that I write, depending on the length of the book.

If you seek the Holy Spirit about financing a book for me, I know that the Lord would be eternally grateful to you. Consider how much this book has blessed you and then think of hundreds or even thousands of people who would be blessed by a book of mine. As you are probably aware, the vast majority of my books are ninety-nine cents on Kindle, which proves to you that book writing is indeed a ministry for me and not a money-making venture. I would be very happy if you supported me in this.

If you have any questions for me or if you want to know what projects I am currently working on that your money might finance, you can write to me at survivors.sanctuary@gmail.com and ask me for more information. I would be pleased to give you more details about my projects.

You can sow any amount to my ministry by simply sending me money via the PayPal link at this address: http://personal-prophecy-today.com/support-my-ministry/

You can be sure that your support, no matter the amount, will be used for the publishing of helpful Christian books for people to read.

Other Books by Matthew Robert Payne

The Prophetic Supernatural Experience

Prophetic Evangelism Made Simple

Your Identity in Christ

His Redeeming Love: A Memoir

Writing and Self-Publishing Christian Nonfiction

Coping with your Pain and Suffering

Living for Eternity

Jesus Speaking Today

Great Cloud of Witnesses Speak

My Radical Encounters with Angels

Finding Intimacy with Jesus Made Simple

My Radical Encounters with Angels: Book Two

A Beginner's Guide to the Prophetic

Michael Jackson Speaks from Heaven

7 Keys to Intimacy with Jesus

Conversations with God: Book 1

Optimistic Visions of Revelation

Conversations with God: Book 2

Finding Your Purpose in Christ

Influencing your World for Christ: Practical Everyday Evangelism

Deep Calls unto Deep: Answering Questions on the Prophetic

My Visits to the Galactic Council of Heaven

The Parables of Jesus Made Simple: Updated and Expanded Edition

Great Cloud of Witnesses Speak: Old and New

Walking under an Open Heaven

A Message from My Angel: Book 1

Interviews with the Two Witnesses: Enoch and Elijah Speak

Gaining Freedom from Sex Addictions: Breaking Free of Pornography and Prostitutes

Mary Magdalene Speaks from Heaven: A Divine Revelation

Princess Diana Speaks from Heaven: A Divine Revelation

How to Hear God's Voice: Keys to Conversational Two-Way Prayer

Apostle John Speaks from Heaven: A Divine Revelation

What I Believe

Great Cloud of Witnesses Speak: God's Generals

Apostle Peter Speaks from Heaven: A Divine Revelation

You can find my published books on my Amazon author page here: http://tinyurl.com/jq3h893

Upcoming Books:

Twenty-Two Signs that You're Called to Be a Prophet

Five Keys to Successful Writing: How I Write One Book per Month

Nineteen Scriptures to Change Your Life Forever: My Life Verses

About Matthew Robert Payne

Matthew was raised in a Baptist church and was led to the Lord at the tender age of eight. He has experienced some pain and darkness in his life, which has given him a deep compassion and love for all people.

Today, he's a founding member and admin of a Facebook group called "Prophetic Training Group," and he invites you to join him there. Matthew has a commission from the Lord to train up prophets and to mentor others in the Christian faith. He does this through his Facebook posts and by writing relevant books on the Christian faith.

God has commissioned him to write at least fifty books in his life, and he spends his days writing and earning the money to self-publish. You can support him by donating money at http://personal-prophecy-today.com or by requesting any of the other services available through his ministry website.

Recently, the Lord has put it on his heart to start his own publishing company for other people's books. It will be called Christian Book Publishing USA. It is Matthew's hope to help some people self-publish their books in the future.

It is Matthew's prayer that this book has blessed you, and he hopes it will lead you into a deeper and more intimate relationship with God.

90

www.ingramcontent.com/pod-product-compliance
Lightning Source LLC
Chambersburg PA
CBHW052111070526
44584CB00017B/2435